SPANISH LANGUAGE
In 25 lessons

Artemiy Belyaev

Edition 1 – January 2018

Copyright © 2016 by Artemiy Belyaev

All rights reserved. This book or any portion thereof may not be reproduced or used in any manner whatsoever without the express written permission of the publisher except for the use of brief quotations in a book review or scholarly journal.

Cover image credit: free image taken from www.pexels.com, the image is licensed under **Creative Commons Zero (CC0) license**.

Spanish usage in the book is checked and corrected by two freelancers - native speaker from Venezuela, and my friend – teacher of Spanish for foreigners from Mexico.

Table of contents

INTRODUCTION 5
HOW TO USE THIS BOOK 5
MAIN DIFFERENCES BETWEEN SPANISH IN SPAIN AND LATIN AMERICA 6
LESSON 1: PRONUNCIATION, RULES OF WRITING AND READING 7
LESSON 2: ARTICLES AND SER, ESTAR – TO BE 10
   GENDER, PLURAL, ARTICLES 10
LESSON 3: VERBS IN PRESENT TENSE 16
   QUESTION WORDS 18
LESSON 4: IRREGULAR VERBS 20
   IRREGULAR VERB SUBGROUPS 20
   VERBS WITH STEM CHANGE 21
LESSON 5: PAST TENSE 24
   PAST TENSE I (IMPERFECTIVE PAST TENSE) 24
   PAST TENSE II (PRETERITE) 26
LESSON 6: FUTURE TENSE, "MUST, TO HAVE TO" 31
   NEAR FUTURE - IR A + INFINITIVE 33
   MUST/TO HAVE TO 33
LESSON 7: PREPOSITIONS 35
   VERBS THAT REQUIRE A PREPOSITION 41
LESSON 8: DIRECT AND INDIRECT OBJECT PRONOUNS 43
   PRONOUNS WITH PREPOSITIONS 47
   THE PERSONAL "A" 47
LESSON 9: MORE PRONOUNS AND IMPORTANT CONSTRUCTIONS 50
   POSSESSIVE PRONOUNS 50
   THE PRONOUN "LO" 51
   SOMETHING, EVERYWHERE, NOBODY ETC. 53
   THIS, THAT, THESE, THOSE 54
   HERE AND THERE 55
LESSON 10: IMPORTANT WORDS AND CONSTRUCTIONS 57
   TODAVÍA, INCLUSO, AÚN, AUN 59
   USE OF MISMO 60
LESSON 11: POR/PARA AND REFLEXIVE VERBS 62
   REFLEXIVE VERBS AND REFLEXIVE PRONOUNS 66
LESSON 12: VERBS LIKE "GUSTAR" AND PASSIVE VOICE 70
   PASSIVE VOICE 72
LESSON 13: CONDITIONAL MOOD AND DEGREES OF COMPARISON 75
   DEGREES OF COMPARISON 76
LESSON 14: IMPERATIVE MOOD 79
   ADVERBS 83

LESSON 15. PROGRESSIVE TENSE AND PRESENT TENSE PARTICIPLES 86
   Other forms progressive tenses 88
LESSON 16: PAST PARTICIPLES, HABER AND PERFECTIVE TENSES 91
   Perfective tenses 92
   The verb HABER 92
   There is/are/were/will be 95
LESSON 17: SUBJUNCTIVE MOOD 97
LESSON 18. PERFECT SUBJUNCTIVE 104
LESSON 19: DIMINUTIVES 107
LESSON 20: IMPORTANT VERBS AND VERBAL CONSTRUCTIONS 108
   How to say "To become" or The verbs of change 108
   The verb VOLVER 110
   The verb DEJAR 111
   LOGRAR, CONSEGUIR, ALCANZAR – to achieve/reach/get 113
   REVISAR, COMPROBAR, VERIFICAR – to check 114
   TRAER and LLEVAR – to bring 115
   SABER and CONOCER 116
   TOMAR and SACAR 117
LESSON 21: GREETINGS AND GOODBYES 118
LESSON 22: THANKS AND APOLOGIZES 120
LESSON 23: HOW TO TELL ABOUT YOURSELF 122
LESSON 24: HOW TO TELL TIME AND DATE? 123
   How to tell a date? 124
LESSON 25: SUMMARIZING, VOCABULARY LEARNING TIPS AND WHAT TO DO FURTHER 125
ADDITIONAL CONTENT 127
   PHRASEBOOK 127
   Verbs that require prepositions 131
   Vocabulary: NUMERALS 134
   Vocabulary: VERBS 136
   Vocabulary: NOUNS 139
   Vocabulary: ADJECTIVES 146
LINKS 148
• FREE BONUS • 148

Introduction

Do you want to speak Spanish? Do you want to know how the Spanish language works, but you don't know where to start?

Then this book is what you are looking for. I created this book to help you to learn Spansih language as fast and easy as possible, to simplify the process and to shorten the learning curve. You finally have a well structured course optimized for self learning.

I have put all my love into this beautiful language into this book, a lot of time and hard work, and I want to express my gratitude towards the people who helped me to learn Spanish, to create this book, who proofread, offered corrections, answered many questions, gave me inspiration and motivation. You guys are great!

How to use this book

This book is designed for Spanish Language learning from absolute zero level. The 25 lessons in this book will walk you through the process of understanding the basics of essential Spanish grammar and learning the vocabulary. Instead of memorizing a lot of common phrases, this book teaches you to build sentences and connect words so that you can build any phrase by yourself, express your thoughts, and hold a conversation, and reach advanced level as soon as possible. What's more, the multiple examples and exercises presented in the book will help you further elevate your Spanish speaking and comprehension skills, thus making the application of what you learn much more effective.

The lessons are ordered by the most appropriate way according to the author. However, feel free to start from whatever lesson you want and jump to whatever lesson you want.

Combine learning with practice. Don't wait to to start using Spanish until you complete all lessons or learn new tense. Start practicing from the beginning. Find study buddies and talk to people.

The section marked "Additional content" contains vocabulary lists with a lot of Spanish words for practicing, and a phrasebook with a lot of common phrases.

Main differences between Spanish in Spain and Latin America

- **The sound "Z"**

In Spain: [th], like in the English word [**th**eater]

In Latin America: [s], like in the English word [**s**oon]

Example: the word *empezar* in Spain sounds as [empe**th**ar], and in Latin America as [empe**s**ar].

- **The sound "C" before I/E**

In Spain: [th]

In Latin America: [s]

Example: the word *conversación* in Spain sounds as [conversa**th**ión], and in Latin America as [conversa**s**ión].

- **Vosotros and Ustedes**

Vosotros and ustedes are plural forms of the pronoun YOU.

In Spain: *vosotros* is the informal plural pronoun YOU and *ustedes* is the formal plural pronoun YOU.

In Latin America: *vosotros* is not used at all and *ustedes* is plural pronoun YOU in all cases.

In this book both pronouns are used.

- **The pronoun Vos**

The pronoun is used only in some countries of Latin America: Paraguay, Uruguay, Argentine, Bolivia. This pronoun equals **tú**. In this book this pronoun will not be considered.

- **Differences in vocabulary.**

Although there are differences in each Spanish speaking country, the differences are not major, so all native speakers perfectly understand each other. It is better to check these differences depending on which country you are interested in.

Lesson 1: Pronunciation, Rules of writing and reading

Aa	Bb	Cc*	Dd	Ee
[c<u>a</u>r]	[<u>b</u>ook]/ [<u>v</u>ote]*	[<u>c</u>art]/ [<u>ce</u>iling]	[<u>d</u>oor]	[st<u>e</u>m]
Ff	Gg	Hh*	Ii	Jj*
[<u>f</u>ocus]	[<u>g</u>ood]	No sound	[kn<u>ee</u>]	[<u>h</u>at]
Kk	Ll*	LL ll	Mm	Nn
[<u>k</u>ey]	[<u>l</u>ove]*	[<u>y</u>our]	[<u>m</u>uch]	[<u>n</u>ame]
Ññ*	Oo	Pp	Qq	Rr*
[ca<u>ny</u>on]	[b<u>o</u>ring]	[<u>p</u>ost]	[<u>q</u>uality]	[<u>r</u>ing]
RR rr*	Ss	Tt	Uu	Vv*
[a<u>rr</u>ogant]	[<u>s</u>oon]	[<u>t</u>ake]	[r<u>u</u>le]	[<u>v</u>ote]/ [<u>b</u>ook]
Ww	Xx	Yy	Zz*	Ch ch
[<u>v</u>ote]	[matri<u>x</u>]	[<u>y</u>our]	[<u>th</u>eater]/ [<u>s</u>oon]	[<u>ch</u>apter]

As you can see, Spanish alphabet is almost the same as English and most sounds are also the same. However, there are nuances with some letters that are marked by *:

- **LL** (double L) and **Y** are pronounced as Y in <u>Y</u>EAR.
- **Y** is pronounced like English Y in [<u>Y</u>EAR]. But only in the single-letter word **Y** – and, consisting from itself is pronounced as EE in [m<u>ee</u>t].
- **G**: before a/o/u is pronounced G as in <u>G</u>AME. Before i/e it is pronounced as H in [<u>h</u>at].
- **J** is pronounced as H in [<u>h</u>at]. Also, J can be used instead of G when in process of conjugation one must place a/o/u after softened G. For example:

Escoge<u>r</u> – to choose, pronounced as [esko<u>h</u>er]

Yo esco<u>j</u>o – I choose, pronounced as [esko<u>h</u>o]

- **Ñ** is soft N. Pronounced as NY in [ca<u>ny</u>on].

7

- **H** doesn't have a sound. This letter is called "Ache". For example, the word *Hablar – to speak* is pronounced as [ablar], and the word *Hijo – son* is pronounced as [eeho].
- **C** before a/o/u sounds like C in [**c**lub], but before i/e sounds like CE in [**ce**iling], as well as in English.
- **Z** has different sounds in Spain and Latin America. In Spain Z sounds like TH in [**th**eater], and in Latil America sounds like S in [**s**oon]. **Also, Z** is used instead of C before e/i when in process of conjugation one must place a/o/u after. For example:

Yo hi**c**e – I did

Él hi**z**o – He did

- **U** is pronounced as U in [r**u**le] or OO in [z**oo**m]
- **U** in **QU, CU, GU** doesn't have a sound. It is used after G, C to keep the sound hard from softening letters i/e. For example, in the word G**u**itarra U is used to keep sound G, because without U this word would sound as "hitarra".
- **Ü** is pronounced as usual OO in Z**OO**M. Used in **QÜ, CÜ, GÜ** when there must be the sound U instead of a diphthong. Example: Vergüenza - shame
- **Qu** – equivalent of C except before a/o/u. Used instead of C when in process of conjugation one must place i/e after C. Example:

Yo to**c**o la guitarra – I play guitar, pronounced [toko]

Yo to**qu**é la guitarra – I played guitar, pronounced [toké]

- **R** – is pronounced as R in English, but with a slight lingual flap.
- **RR** – is pronounced as strong rolled R.
- **K, W** – equivalents of C, V, they are used only in loan words.
- **Ch** equals English CH as in **CH**AT.
- **B** and **V** don't have a difference in pronunciation. Spanish speakers pronounce these sounds either as B or as V depending on local accent, or as a sound between both of these letters.

Stressed syllables

If a word ends on a vowel and on the consonants N, S – the accent is on the penultimate syllable, e.g. EST_A_BAN, if a word ends on a consonant apart from N, S – the accent is on the last syllable, e.g. NACION_A_L.

If the accent doesn't fit these rules – there must be an accent mark above, e.g. ESTÁ.

Also, the accent mark is written in some words to distinguish their meaning: SÍ – yes, SI – if, QUÉ – what, QUE – than, that, ÉL – he, EL – definite article, and others.

Read these words now and build sentences with them after the next lesson:

Gracias – thanks [grásias]

Hola – hello [óla]

Humano – human [umáno]

Mañana – morning/tomorrow [manyána]

Amor – love [amór]

Practicar – to practice [practicár]

Carretera – road [carretéra]

Español – Spanish [espaniól]

Lluvia – rain [yúvia]

Difícil – difficult [difícil]

Carretera – road [carretéra]

Hamster – hamster [ámster]

Incredible – increíble [increíbleh]

Plaza – square [plátha (Spain)/plása (LA)]

Amarillo – yellow [amaríyo]

Zapatos – shoes [thapátos (Spain)/sapatos (LA)]

Joven – young [hóven]

Llamar – to call [yamár]

Rechazar – to reject [rechathár (Spain), Rechasár (LA)]

Ser – to be [ser]

Estar – to be [estár]

Dibujar – to draw [dibuhár]

Empezar – to start/begin [empethár (Spain), empesár (LA)]

Hijo – son [éeho]

Hija – daughter [éeha]

Lápiz – pencil [lápith (Spain)/lapis(LA)]

Quierer – to want [querér]

Vergüenza – shame [verguéntha (Spain)/[verguénsa (LA)]

9

Lesson 2: Articles and SER, ESTAR – to be

Gender, plural, articles

As it was said before, Spanish is a gender-based language. All nouns and adjectives belong to a gender. There are 2 grammatical genders in the Spanish language: masculine and feminine. Grammatical gender is not a physical gender, it means different things.

The plural form is formed by adding –S or –ES to an ending, as well as in English.

- **Masculine nouns** usually end in: Consonants, -O, -E, and there are some words in –A.

Every noun has an article that denounces a gender.

Masculine articles (indefinite, definite):

Un (singular), unos (plural) – indefinite articles

El (singular), los (plural) – definite articles

Some examples:

Un amigo – a friend (male)

El gato – cat

Un perro – a dog

El humano – human

Los humanos – humans

Un chico – a guy/boy

- **Feminine nouns** usually end in: -A, -DAD, -CIÓN.

Feminine articles (indefinite, definite):

Una (singular), Unas (plural) – indefinite articles

La (singular), las (plural) – definite articles

Some examples:

La amiga – friend (female)

La familia – family

La diseñadora – designer (female)

La lección – lesson

Las carreteras – roads

Una chica – a girl

Unas canciónes – songs

- **Also**, there are nouns that end in **–E and –ISTA** – they can be either masculine or feminine and they may have a plural form – just by adding –S.

El/la periodista, los/las periodistas – journalist(s)

El/la ciclista, los/las ciclistas – cyclist(s)

El/la deportista, los/las deportistas – sportsman(s)

There are exceptions when an ending doesn't determine gender:

la foto – photo	el día – day	el problema – problem
el mapa – map	el sofá – sofa	el programa – program
la radio – radio	el alma – soul	el sistema – system
la mano – hand	el tranvía – tram	el diploma – diploma
el clima – climate	el planeta – planet	el políglota – polyglot

- **Spanish adjectives** are divided into two types:

Adjectives that have gender ending **–O (masculine) or –A (feminine)** change gender and number:

Buen**o** – good (masculine), Buen**a** – good (feminine)

El bosque hermos**o** – beautiful (masculine) forest

La montaña hermos**a** – beautiful (feminine) mountain

Los árboles cortos – short (masculine, plural) trees

And adjectives that have **all other endings,** they change only number:

Grande (singular), grande**s** (plural) – big

Interesante (singular), interesante**s** (plural) – interesting

La gente joven – Young people (singular)

Las chicas jóvene**s** – Young girls (plural)

Ser and Estar – to be

There are two verbs "to be" in Spanish language – SER and ESTAR. With the help of these verbs we can say "I am, you are, he is" and so on. The difference between SER and ESTAR is:

- **SER** is used to indicate a **constant state**, for example: name, occupation, profession, origin, nationality, relation, time, date, identity, permanent characteristic, physical description, location of an event.
- **ESTAR** is used to indicate a **temporal state**, for example: temporal location, status, activity, health, position, emotion, temporary condition.

These verbs are irregular, so their conjugation should just be memorized.

Conjugation of the verb **SER** – to be:

Yo soy	I am
Tú eres	You are
Él es	He is
Ella es	She is
Usted es	You are (formal)
Nosotros(-as) somos	We are
Vosotros(-as) sois	You are (plural)
Ellos(-as) son	They are
Ustedes son	You are (formal, plural)

What are (-AS) endings? Spanish is a gender-based language. One says **nosotros** when the speakers are male or mixed-gender groups, and one says **nosotras** when the speakers are female. The same with **vosotros** and **vosotras**, **ellos** and **ellas**.

Usted is a formal (polite) pronoun *you*, and *ustedes* is plural formal pronoun *you*. In most of countries of Latin America *ustedes* is used as plural *you* instead of vosotros. *Vosotros* is used widely only in Spain.

Conjugation of the verb **ESTAR** – to be

Yo estoy	I am
Tú estás	You are
Él está	He is
Ella está	She is
Usted está	You are (formal)
Nosotros(-as) estamos	We are
Vosotros(-as) estáis	You are (plural)
Ellos(-as) están	They are
Ustedes están	You are (formal, plural)

Examples

Ser joven – *To be young*
Yo soy joven – I am young
Él es joven – He is young
Ellos son jóvenes – They are young

Estar sano – *To be healthy*
Él está sano – He is healthy
Ella está sana – She is healthy

Ser de Costa Rica – *To be from Costa Rica*
Ellos son de Costa Rica – They are from Costa Rica

Estar ocupado – *to be busy*
Nosotros estamos ocupados – We are busy
Ella está ocupada – She is busy
Usted es ocupado – You are busy

Estar enfermo – *to be ill*
Él está enfermo – he is ill
Ella está enferma – They are ill
Ellas están enfermas – They (females) are ill

Yo soy actor – I am an actor

Nosotros estamos ocupados – we are busy

Lucila es maestra – Lucila is a teacher

Ellos están en la lección – they are at the lesson

Ellas son lindas – they are cute (females)

El pelo es oscuro – the hair is dark

Los hamsters no son rápidos – the hamsters are not fast

El libro está en la biblioteca – the book is in the library

Vosotros estáis sanos – you are healthy

¿Estás contento? – are you glad?

Ella es pequeña – she is short

Ellos son libres - they are free

Las ciudades son grandes – the cities are big

Ella es maestra y está ocupada ahora – She is a teacher and (she) is busy now

Mi hermana está en aeropuerto – My sister is in airport

Javier es de Venezuela – Javier is from Venezuela

Fernando está listo – Fernando is ready

La música es rudiosa – The music is loud

La botella está vacía – The bottle is empty

Build sentences with these nouns and adjectives using all that you learned in this lesson:

ocupado – busy	el humano – human,	el diseñador – designer,
bueno – good	la carretera – road	la amiga – friend (female)
lindo – cute	la familia – family	el amigo – friend (male)
rápido – fast	la camisa – shirt	interesante – interesting
oscuro – dark	contento – glad	el maestro – teacher (male)
el chico – guy	la lección – lesson	la maestra – teacher (female)
la chica – girl	hermoso – beautiful	la biblioteca – library
corto – short	el hermano – brother	grande – big
libre – free	la hermana – sister	

Exercises

A. Use an appropriate definite article EL, LOS, LA, LAS:
1. ___ cama – the bed;
2. ___ camisa – the shirt;
3. ___ biblioteca – the library;
4. ___ niño – the child;
5. ___ ojos – the eyes;
6. ___ playas – the beaches;
7. ___ soldado – the soldier;
8. ___ niñas – the children

B. Use the verb SER or ESTAR in appropriate form of conjugation:
1. Él ___ en Argentina – He is in Argentine
2. Los niños ___ muy amables – The children are very lovely
3. Marco y su mujer no ___ ocupados – Marco and his wife are not busy
4. Nosotros ___ estudiantes de la universidad – We are students of the university
5. Ella ___ mi hermana – She is my sister
6. ¿Vosotros ___ en el teatro? – Are you in the theatre?
7. ¿Usted ___ de España? – Are You from Spain?
8. ¿Dónde (tú) ___ ahora? – Where are you now?
9. ¿Quién (tú) ___ ? – Who are you?
10. ¿De dónde ___ ? – Where are you from?

C. Use the adjective in appropriate gender and number
1. Mis hermanos son ___ (ALTO - tall) – My brothers are tall
2. Esta señora es ___ (BELLO - beautiful) – This lady is beautiful
3. Los gatos son muy ___ (LINDO - cute) – The cats are very cute
4. Estes libros son ___ (INTERESANTE – interesting) – These books are interesting
5. La casa es ___ (VERDE - green) – The house is green
6. El sol es ___ (BRILLANTE – bright) – The sun is bright

Answers:
A. **1**: la, **2**: la, **3**: la, **4**: el, **5**: los, **6**: las, **7**: el, **8**: las.
B. **1**: está, **2**: son, **3**: están, **4**: somos, **5**: es, **6**: estáis, **7**: es, **8**: estás, **9**: eres, **10**: eres
C. **1**: altos, **2**: bella, **3**: lindos, **4**: interesantes, **5**: verde, **6**: brillante

Lesson 3: Verbs in present tense

There are 3 types of verbs in the Spanish language; they have the endings **–AR, -ER, -IR** in infinitive forms.

Let's conjugate the verbs *preguntar – to ask, vender – to sell, abrir – to open* in Present tense and look at the endings.

Preguntar – to ask, this verb is from **–AR** group

Yo pregunt<u>o</u>	I ask
Tú pregunt<u>as</u>	You ask
Él, ella pregunt<u>a</u>	He, she asks
Usted pregunt<u>a</u>	You ask (formal)
Nosotros(-as) pregunt<u>amos</u>	We ask
Vosotros(-as) pregunt<u>áis</u>	You ask (plural)
Ellos(-as) pregunt<u>an</u>	They ask
Ustedes pregunt<u>an</u>	You ask (formal, plural)

All regular verbs of – AR group will have these endings with each of the pronouns. The –AR group is the largest, about 85% of Spanish verbs belong to this group.

Vender – to sell, this verb is from **–ER** group

Yo vend<u>o</u>	I sell
Tú vend<u>es</u>	You sell
Él, ella vend<u>e</u>	He, she sells
Usted vend<u>e</u>	You sell (formal)
Nosotros(-as) vend<u>imos</u>	We sell
Vosotros(-as) vend<u>éis</u>	You sell (plural)
Ellos(-as) vend<u>en</u>	They sell
Ustedes vend<u>en</u>	You sell (plural, formal)

All regular –ER verbs will have these endings with each pronoun. There are also irregular verbs that will be considered in the next lesson.

Abrir – to open, this verb is from **–IR** group

Yo abr<u>o</u>	I open
Tú abr<u>es</u>	You open
Él, ella abr<u>e</u>	He, she opens
Usted abr<u>e</u>	You open (plural)
Nosotros(-as) abr<u>imos</u>	We open
Vosotros(-as) abr<u>ís</u>	You open (plural)
Ellos(-as) abr<u>en</u>	They open
Ustedes abr<u>en</u>	You open (formal, plural)

All regular –IR verbs will have these endings.

There are many irregular verbs that have their own forms at conjugation, but we will consider them in the next lesson.

Conjugate these regular verbs in Present tense with all pronouns using the templates above:

-AR: Contestar – to answer, Hablar – to speak, Saltar – to jump, Amar – to love, Viajar – to travel, Cantar – to sing, Tomar – to take, Trabajar – to work, Estudiar – to study, Aprender – to learn, Comprar – to buy, Bailar – to dance, Enseñar – to teach, Buscar – to seek, Necesitar – to need.

-ER: Comer – to eat, Beber – to drink, Leer – to read, Comprender – to understand, Creer – to believe, Cometer – commit.

-IR: Vivir – to live, Escribir – to write, Describir – to describe, Compartir – to share, Recibir – to receive, Aburrir – to bore.

Examples

¿Tú vives en España? – Do you live in Spain?

Ella lee un libro – She reads a book

Él está ocupado cuando trabaja – He is busy when he works

No pueden hablar inglés – They can't speak English

María bebe un café – Maria drinks a coffee

¿Quiere usted probar la comida española? – Do you want to try Spanish food?

Tú cantas muy bien – You sing very good

Ella toma much<u>as</u> fotos – She takes many pictures

El bolígrafo no escribe bien – The pen doesn't write well

Yo necesito aprender español en la universidad – I need to study Spanish in the university

Question words

¿Qué? – what?

¿Quién(es)? – who?

¿De quién (es)? – whose?

¿Cómo? – how?

¿Dónde? – where?

¿Adónde? – to where?

¿De dónde? – from where?

¿Cuál(es)? – which?*

¿Cuándo? – when?*

¿Cuánto? – how much?

¿Cuántos? – how many?

¿Por qué? – why?

¿Para qué? – why? what for?

*- One must use stress mark with these question words only in questions and exclamations

Examples

¿Cuándo vas a dormir? – When you go to sleep?

¿Por qué cierras la puerta? – Why do you close the door?

¿Dónde juegas al fútbol? – Where do you play football?

¿Qué no entiendes? – What don't you understand?

¿Cómo piensas? – How do you think?

Exercises

Conjugate verbs in present tense.

1. Él _____ una cerveza todos los días (BEBER – *to drink*) – He drinks a beer every day
2. Ellas _____ en la tienda (TRABAJAR – *to work*) – They(females) work in the store
3. Nosotras _____ con la gente (HABLAR – *to speak*) – We(females) speak with the people
4. _____ hablar más (NECESITAR – *to need*) – We need to speak more
5. Tú y yo _____ juntos (BAILAR – *to dance*) – I and you dance together
6. ¿Por qué (tú) no _____ mis preguntas? (CONTESTAR – *to answer*) – Why you don't answer my questions?
7. Anna y Caterina _____ un trabajo (BUSCAR – *to look for*) – Anna and Catherine look for a job
8. ¿Vosotros _____ un periódico? (LEER – *to read*) – Do you read a newspaper?
9. ¿Por qué tú _____ tantas manzanas? (COMER – *to eat*) – Why do you eat so many apples?
10. ¿Cómo ustedes _____ acá? (VIVIR – *to live*) – How do You live here?
11. El gato _____ a la mesa (SALTAR – *to jump*) – The cat jumps onto the table
12. El professor _____ un sujeto a los estudiantes (EXPLICAR – *to explain*) – The professor explains the subject to the students
13. ¿Por qué ustedes _____ aquí? (CAMINAR – *to walk*) – Why do you walk here?
14. ¿Quién de ustedes _____ a hablar Español? (APRENDER – *to learn*) – Who of you learns to speak Spanish?
15. ¿Qué Usted _____ en el colegio? (ESTUDIAR – *to study*) – What do You study in the college?

Answers

1: bebe, **2**: trabajan, **3**: hablamos, **4**: necesitamos, **5**: bailamos, **6**: contestas, **7**: buscan, **8**: leéis, **9**: comes, **10**: viven, **11**: salta, **12**: explica, **13**: caminan, **14**: aprende, **15**: estudia

Lesson 4: Irregular verbs

In this lesson we will consider Spanish irregular verbs: irregular subgroups of –ER and –IR verbs, verbs with stem change and exceptional irregular verbs that must be only memorized.

IR – to go, TENER – to have, QUERER – to want/to love, HACER – to do and other irregular verbs and their common characteristics.

Irregular verb subgroups

- **Subgroups –CER and -CIR:**

-CER is a subgroup of –ER group, and –CIR is a subgroup of –IR group. Verbs ending in –CER or –CIR end in –ZCO in conjugation with the pronoun YO:

Conocer – to know, Yo conozco – I know

Aparecer – to appear, Yo aparezco – I appear

Parecer – to look like, Yo parezco – I know

Ofrecer – to offer, Yo ofrezco – I offer

Seducir – to seduce, Yo seduzco – I seduce

Producir – to produce, Yo produzco – I produce

Reducir – to reduce, Yo reduzco – I reduce

With all other pronouns they have ordinary form, e.g. *tú conoces, él conoce, nosotros conocemos* and so on.

- **Subgroups –NER and –NIR:**

-NER is a subrgoup of –ER verbs, and –NIR is a subgroup of –IR group. Verbs with these infinitive endings will end in –GO in conjugation with the pronoun YO:

Tener – to have, Yo tengo – I have

Venir – to come, Yo vengo – I come

Poner – to put, Yo pongo – I put

Suponer – to suppose, Yo supongo – I suppose

Proponer – to propose, Yo propongo – I propose

Verbs with stem change

There are plenty of irregular verbs that have a change in stem *in present tense*. These changes are: E – IE, U – UE, O – UE, E-I. They are applied for all pronouns apart from *nosotros* and *vosotros*.

T<u>e</u>ner – to have. This verb has -NER, so the conjugation with YO will be "TENGO" instead of ~~tieno~~, and E-IE change in stem (apart from Nosotros and Vosotros as it was said before).

Yo tengo	I have (own form with *yo*)
Tú t<u>ie</u>nes	You have
Él, ella, usted t<u>ie</u>ne	He, she, you have
Nosotros tenemos	We have
Vosotros tenéis	You have
Ellos, ustedes t<u>ie</u>nen	They, you have

Qu<u>e</u>rer – to want/to love. This verb has E-IE change in stem.

Yo qu<u>ie</u>ro	I want
Tú qu<u>ie</u>res	You want
Él, ella, usted qu<u>ie</u>re	He, she, you want
Nosotros queremos	We want
Vosotros queréis	You want
Ellos, ustedes qu<u>ie</u>ren	They, you want

Other irregular verbs with stems in present tense:

	Change	Stem
Dormir– to sleep	o-ue	Duerm-
Jugar – to play	u-ue	Jueg-
Entender– to understand	e-ie	Entiend-
Costar – to cost	o-ue	Cuest-
Pensar – to think	e-ie	Piens-
Encontrar – to find	o-ue	Encuentr-

Pedir – to ask for	e-i	Pid-
Perder – to lose	e-ie	Pierd-
Cerrar – to close	e-ei	Cierr-
Volver – to return	o-ue	Vuelv-
Recordar – to remember	o-ue	Recuerd-

Exceptional irregular verbs

First of all – the verb **IR** – to go. This verb has own forms of conjugation with all pronouns that must be memorized.

Ir – to go

Yo voy	I go
Tú vas	You go
Él, ella, usted va	He, she goes, you go
Nosotros vamos	We go
Vosotros váis	You go
Ellos, ustedes van	They, you go

Hacer – to do. This verb has the only irregular form "Yo hago".

Yo hago	I do
Tú haces	You do
Él, ella, usted hace	He, she does, you do
Nosotros hacemos	We do
Vosotros hacéis	You do
Ellos hacen	They do

Decir – to say. Despite the fact that this verb has –CIR, this one is fully exceptional:

Yo digo	I say
Tú dices	You say
Él, ella, usted dice	He, she says, you say

Nosotros decimos	We say
Vosotros decís	You say
Ellos dicen	They say

Saber – to know (something)
Yo sé – I know. This is the only irregular form.

Dar – to give
Yo doy – I give. The only irregular form.

Ver – to see
Yo veo – I see. The only irregular form.

Oír – to hear
Yo oigo, tu oyes, el oye, nosotros oímos, vosotros oís, ellos oyen.

Salir – to leave
Yo salgo – I leave. The only irregular form

Caer – to fall
Yo caigo – I fall. The only irregular form

Traer – to bring
Yo traigo – I bring. The only irregular form

Oler – to smell
Yo huelo, tú hueles, él huele, nosotros olemos, vosotros oléis, ellos huelen

Build sentences with these words and irregular verbs that you learned in this lesson:

la canción – song	la pared – wall	el emprendedor – entrepreneur
la oficina – office	el amor – love	
el dinero – money	la voz – voice	el directór – director
el camión – truck	la copa – glass	la cámara – camera
el corazón – heart	el juego – game	el trabajador – employee

Conjugate these verbs in present tense with all pronouns:

conducir – to drive	traducir - to translate
establecer – to establish	nacer – to be born
reconocer – to recognize	crecer – to grow

Lesson 5: Past tense

In this lesson we will consider two past tenses of the Spanish language.

Past tense I (Imperfective past tense)

This tense refers to an action in the past that has an indefinite (unknown) start and end date, continued or repeated action, started in the past and continues in the present, or took place over a period of time.

In simple words, it can be an action that was performed in the past but is not finished yet, or was performed often or sometimes, or many times, i.e. repeatedly. It could be 1,000 years ago, or 1 day ago, or the action could be started some minutes ago, i.e. the time range doesn't matter. Some examples in English: "I walked there often", "Sometimes he smoked", "We watched this film many times", "They go there every year".

Some keywords for this tense:	
Siempre – always	A veces – sometimes
A menudo – often	Cada año – every year
Frecuentemente – frequently	Mucho – a lot

Now let's see how to conjugate verbs in this tense, and then consider examples.

Escuch<u>ar</u> – to listen to

Yo escuch<u>aba</u>	I listened
Tú escuch<u>abas</u>	You listened
Él, ella, usted escuch<u>aba</u>	He, she, you listened
Nosotros escuch<u>ábamos</u>	We listened
Vosotros escuch<u>abais</u>	You listened
Ellos, ustedes escuch<u>aban</u>	They, you listened

All regular **–AR** verbs will have these endings in this tense.

−ER and **−IR** verbs have the same forms of conjugation in this tense.

Dormir – to sleep (regular in this tense)

Yo dormía	I slept
Tú dormías	You slept
Él, ella, usted dormía	He, she, you slept
Nosotros dormíamos	We slept
Vosotros dormíais	You slept
Ellos, ustedes dormían	They, you slept

All regular –ER and –IR verbs will have these endings in this tense.

Almost all verbs are regular in this tense. However, the verbs SER – to be, and IR – to go, and VER – to see are not. So their conjugation just has to be memorized:

	Ser – to be	**Ir** – to go	**Ver** – to see
Yo	era	iba	veía
Tú	eras	ibas	veías
Él, ella, usted	era	iba	veía
Nosotros	éramos	íbamos	veíamos
Vosotros	erais	ibais	veíais
Ellos, ustedes	eran	iban	veían

Conjugate these verbs in this tense:

Tener – to have   Explicar – to explain   Poder – can
Dibujar – to draw   Tratar – to try   Vivir – to live
Pensar – to think   Traer – to bring   Oír – to hear

Examples

Ellos hablaban Inglés a veces – They spoke English sometimes

Nosotros comíamos mucho la comida Española – We ate Spanish food a lot

Yo dormía por un rato – I slept for a while

Ustedes no escuchaban la música – You didn't listen to the music

Cuando tú eras joven, ¡Estudiabas mucho! – When you were young, you used to study a lot!

¿Adónde iba usted todo el tiempo? – Where did you go all the time?

Ellas visitaban la exhibición a menudo – They (females) visited the exhibition often

Alberto veía la ciudad a menudo – Albert saw the city often

Ella hacía compras en la tienda – She made purchases in the store

Yo estaba en la escuela todos los días – I have been to school every day

Past tense II (Preterite)

Unlike the *past tense I*, this tense refers to an action with definite (known) period of time, an action that occurred in the past and was finished, or continues until now.

Some keywords for this tense:	
Ayer – yesterday,	La semana pasada – last week
Anteayer – the day before yesterday	El otro día – the other day
Una vez – once	Hace … años - … years ago
El año pasado – last year	Anoche – last night

Now let's see how to conjugate verbs in this tense.

Invitar – to invite

Yo invit__é__	I invited
Tú invit__aste__	You invited
Él, ella, usted invit__ó__	He, she, you invited
Nosotros invit__amos__	We invited
Vosotros invit__asteis__	You invited
Ellos, ustedes invit__aron__	They, you invited

All regular –AR verbs will have these endings in this tense.

As you can see, the conjugation with **nosotros** matches with its conjugation in the present tense.

In this tense –ER and –IR verbs have the same endings.

Responder – to respond

Yo respond<u>í</u>	I responded
Tú respond<u>iste</u>	You responded
Él, ella, usted respind<u>ió</u>	He, she, You responded
Nosotros respond<u>imos</u>	We responded
Vosotros respond<u>isteis</u>	You responded
Ellos, ustedes respond<u>ieron</u>	They, You responded

All regular –ER and –IR verbs will have these endings in this tense.

*The **examples** will be after the next section "irregular verbs"*

Conjugate these verbs in both past tenses with all pronouns:

Ocurrir – to occur
Llamar – to call
Leer- to read
Soñar – to dream
Aceptar – to accept
Permitir – to permit
Manejar – to drive
Dar – to give

Prestar – to borrow
Cancelar – to cancel
Cambiar – to change
Terminar – to finish
Lograr – to achieve/accomplish
Pasar – to pass/to happen
Aparecer – to appear
Quejar – to complain

Build sentences with these words:

la calle – street
la mesa – table
la escuela – school
el colegio – college
el minuto – minute
el segundo – second
el bolleto – ticket
la práctica – practice
juntos – together
el bolígrafo – pen

el avión – airplane
barato – cheap
caro – expensive
amable – kind
caliente – hot
peligroso – dangerous
completo – complete
frecuente – frequent
el libro – book
la ciudad – city/town

el día – day
lejos – far
la hora – hour
el año – year
cerca – close
el lápiz – pencil
seguro – safe
pasado – past
el mes – month
la semana – week

27

Irregular verbs

Before considering examples, let's learn more about irregular verbs in this tense. First of all – SER and IR. And there is a surprise – these two verbs have the same form in this tense!

Ser – to be, **ir** – to go

Yo fui	I went, i was
Tú fuiste	You went, you were
Él, ella, usted fue	He, she, you went, were
Nosotros fuimos	We went, we were
Vosotros fuisteis	You went, you were
Ellos, ustedes fueron	They went, you were

Unfortunately, there are a lot of irregular verbs in the Spanish language. Let's consider the most often used ones.

	Tener - to have	**Estar** - to be	**Hacer** - to do
Yo	tuve	estuve	hice
Tú	tuviste	estuviste	hiciste
Él, ella, usted	tuvo	estuvo	hizo
Nosotros	tuvimos	estuvimos	hicimos
Vosotros	tuvisteis	estuvisteis	hicisteis
Ellos, ustedes	tuvieron	estuvieron	hicieron

Notice, that in the irregular verbs the endings with Yo and Él, Ella, Usted are not stressed unlike the regular verbs!

Also:

Quierer – to want, stem: QUIS-, Yo quise

Saber – to know, stem: SUP-, Yo supe

Poder – can, stem: PUD-, Yo pude

Decir – to say, stem DIJ-, yo dije

Dar – to give, stem: D-, Yo di

Traducir – to translate, stem: TRADUJ-, yo traduje

Poner – to put, stem: PUS-, yo puse

Venir – to come, stem: VIN-, yo vine

Dormir – to sleep, stem with Él, Ella, Ud., Ellos, Uds.: DURM-: Él durmió, ellos durmieron

Examples

¿Qué pasó? – What happened?

Yo fui un director – I was a director

Nosotros tratamos de cantar ayer – We tried to sing yesterday

El año pasado Pedro estudió la informática – Pedro studied IT last year

Ella fue al teatro anteayer – She went to the theater the day before yesterday

Nosotros tuvimos los boletos – We had the tickets

¿Vosotros estuvisteis en la conferencia hace una hora? – Have you been to the conference one hour ago?

¿Ustedes practicaron el paracaidismo una vez? – Did you practice skydiving once?

¿Dónde estuviste ayer? – Where were you yesterday?

Este político dijo otras cosas hace ocho años – This politician said other things eight years ago

¿Que bebieron Ustedes en el bar? – What did you drink in the bar?

¿Dónde estuvisteis anoche? – Where were you last night?

¿Con quién bailaste en la fiesta? – With whom did you dance in the party?

¿Por qué saliste temprano? – Why did you leave early?

Yo descargué una programa – I downloaded a program

No supieron nada sobre eso – They didn't know anything about that

Exercises

Conjugate verbs in appropriate past tense.

1. Juan y Maria _____ acá a menudo (CAMINAR – to walk) – Juan and Maria walked here often
2. ¿Qué _____ allí ayer? (OCCURRIR – *to occur*) – What occurred there yesterday?
3. Ellos _____ a menudo la comida española (comer – *to eat*) – They ate Spanish food often
4. Yo le _____ poco dinero a de mi amigo anteayer (PRESTAR – to borrow) – I borrowed a little money from my friend the day before yesterday
5. Mi madre y yo no lo _____ nunca (SABER – to know) – My mother and I never knew it.
6. ¿Quién _____ el dinero? (TENER – to have) – Who had the money?
7. Mi amigo _____ mucho en mi casa (DORMIR – to sleep) – My friend slept in my home many times
8. El hombre _____ a alguien en la calle hace cinco minutos (LLAMAR – to call) – The man called somebody in the street five minutes ago
9. El juego _____ bueno hoy (SER - to be) – The game was good today
10. Los niños a veces _____ en la habitación (JUGAR – to play) – The children played in the room sometimes
11. Los doctores _____ que ella estaba sano (PENSAR – to think) – The doctors thought that she is healthy
12. ¿Qué canción _____ hace un minuto? (ESCUCHAR – to listen) – Which song did you(Tú) listen one minute ago?
13. ¿Por qué ella _____ a la tienda tan a menudo? (IR- to go) – What did she go to the store so often?
14. Pedro _____ ingeniero por un largo tiempo (SER – to be) – He was an engineer for long time

Answers

1: caminaban, **2**: occurrió, **3**: comían, **4**: presté, **5**: supimos, **6**: tenía, **7**: dormía, **8**: llamó, **9**: fue, **10**: jugaban, **11**: pensaron, **12**: escuchaste, **13**: iba, **14**: era

Lesson 6: Future tense, "Must, to have to"

Future tense is the easiest tense in Spanish language, because there is no difference between –AR, -ER, -IR verbs in this tense; they all will have the same endings.

Saltar – to jump

Yo saltar**é**	I will jump
Tú saltar**ás**	You will jump
Él, ella, usted saltar**á**	He, she, you will jump
Nosotros saltar**emos**	We will jump
Vosotros saltar**éis**	You will jump
Ellos, ustedes saltar**án**	They, you will jump

All regular –AR, -ER, -IR verbs will have these endings in the future tense.

The verbs SER and IR are regular in this tense, however it is better to check their conjugate in order not to get confused with it:

	Ser – to be	**Ir** - to go
Yo	ser**é**	ir**é**
Tú	ser**ás**	ir**ás**
Él, ella, usted	ser**é**	ir**é**
Nosotros	ser**emos**	ir**emos**
Vosotros	ser**áis**	ir**éis**
Ellos, ustedes	ser**án**	ir**án**

Also, there are irregular verbs in this tense, they have the same endings, but another stem.

Irregular verbs:

Tener – to have, stem: TENDR-

Hacer – to do, stem: HAR-

Querer – to want, stem: QUERR-

Poder – can, stem: PODR-

Poner – to put, stem: PONDR-

Saber – to know, stem: SABR-

Decir – to say, stem: DIR-

Venir – to come, stem: VENDR-

Salir – to leave, stem: SALDR-

Examples

Yo iré a la plaza – I will go to the square

Nosotros querremos comer – We will want to eat

David traducirá el texto mañana – David will translate the text tomorrow

¿Tomarás las manzanas del árbol? – Will you take apples from the tree?

Un artista dibujará la imagen de nosotros – An artist will draw an image of us

¿Me amarás por siempre? – Will you love me forever?

Dos hermanos irán a la escuela juntos mañana – Two brother will go to school together tomorrow

Vendremos a la oficina en una hora – We will come to the office in one hour

¿Qué Usted hará si tiene un millón? – What will you do if you have a million?

Despues del entrenamiento sabréis muchas cosas – After the training you will know many things

Conjugate these regular verbs in future tense with all pronouns:

Acordar – to agree
Planificar – to plan
Afectar – to affect
Impactar – to impact
Cocinar – to cook
Discutir – to discuss
Contar – to tell

Reparar – to repair
Descansar – to rest
Construir – to build
Traducir – to translate
Mostrar – to show
Mirar – to watch/ to look
Abrazar – to hug

Near future - IR A + INFINITIVE

There is one more form of the future tense. In the English language we can say "to be going to do something", "I am going to do something", in Spanish this construction is almost the same.

IR A + INFINITIVE means "to be going to ..... (do something)", i.e. in the near future. (IR is conjugated in the appropriate tense)

Examples

¿Quién va a venir aquí? – Who is going to come here?

Miguel iba a servir en el ejército – Miguel was going to serve in army

Mañana ella irá a empezar a hacer deporte – Tomorrow she will be going to start to do sport

La manufactura va a producir cien muestras – The manufacture is going to produce one hundred sample

¿Cuándo van a salir? – When are they going to leave?

Must/to have to

- **Tener que** – to have to

Tengo que cocinar la comida por la tarde – I have to cook the food for the evening

¿Qué tienes que hacer hoy? – What do you have to do today?

- **Deber** – must

Debemos saberlo – We must know it

Debe estar aquí – it must be here

- **Hay que** – one must (passive form)

Hay que tener un pasaporte – One must have a passport

Hay que mantener la paciencia – One must keep patience

Build sentences with these words:

la plaza – square	facíl – easy	la casa – home/house,
la iglesia – church	el auto – car	el traductor - translator
la botella – bottle	el tren – train	la autopista – highway
el salario – salary	la puerta – door	la carretera – road
la televición – TV	el trabajo – work	la estación – station
la bicicleta – bicycle	el autobús – bus	la habitación – room

Exercises
Conjugate verbs in future tense

1. Él _____ la tarea antes de mañana (HACER – to do) – He will do this task before tomorrow
2. Yo _____ la botella en la mesa (PONER – to put) – I will put the bottle onto the table
3. Mi padre _____ una tequila de Mexico (TRAER – to bring) – My father will bring a tequila from Mexico
4. ¿Cuándo Diana _____ acá? (VENIR – to come) – When Diana come here?
5. Los maesteros _____ nuestras bicicletas (REPARAR – to repair) – The masters will repair our bicycles
6. La maestra _____ este tema (EXPLICAR – to explain) – The teacher will explain this subject
7. El avión _____ a los Estados Unidos (VOLAR – to fly) – The airplane will fly to the United States
8. ¿_____ a un bar despues del trabajo? (IR – to go) – Will you (tú) go to a bar after work?
9. ¿Te _____ para el examen? (PREPARAR – to prepare) – Will you (Vosotros) prepare for the exam?
10. ¿_____ mi salario o no? (AFECTAR – to affect) – Will it affect my salary or no?
11. Nosotros _____ al aeropuerto pronto (LLEGAR – to arrive) – We will arrive to the airport soon
12. El sacerdote _____ a la iglesia (SERVIR – to serve) – The priest will serve in the church
13. Ella _____ hasta las ocho (TRABAJAR – to work) – She will work until 8.
14. El clima* _____ bueno mañana - The weather will be good tomorrow (SER – to be; *-el clima - masculine exception with the ending -A)
15. ¿_____ a tu madre mañana? (LLAMAR – to call) – Will you(Tú) call your mother tomorrow?

Answers
1: hará, **2**: pondré, **3**: traerá, **4**: vendrá, **5**: repararán, **6**: explicará, **7**: volará, **8**: irás, **9**: prepararáis, **10**: afectará, **11**: llegaremos, **12**: servirá, **13**: trabajará, **14**: será, **15**: llamarás

Lesson 7: Prepositions

Place.

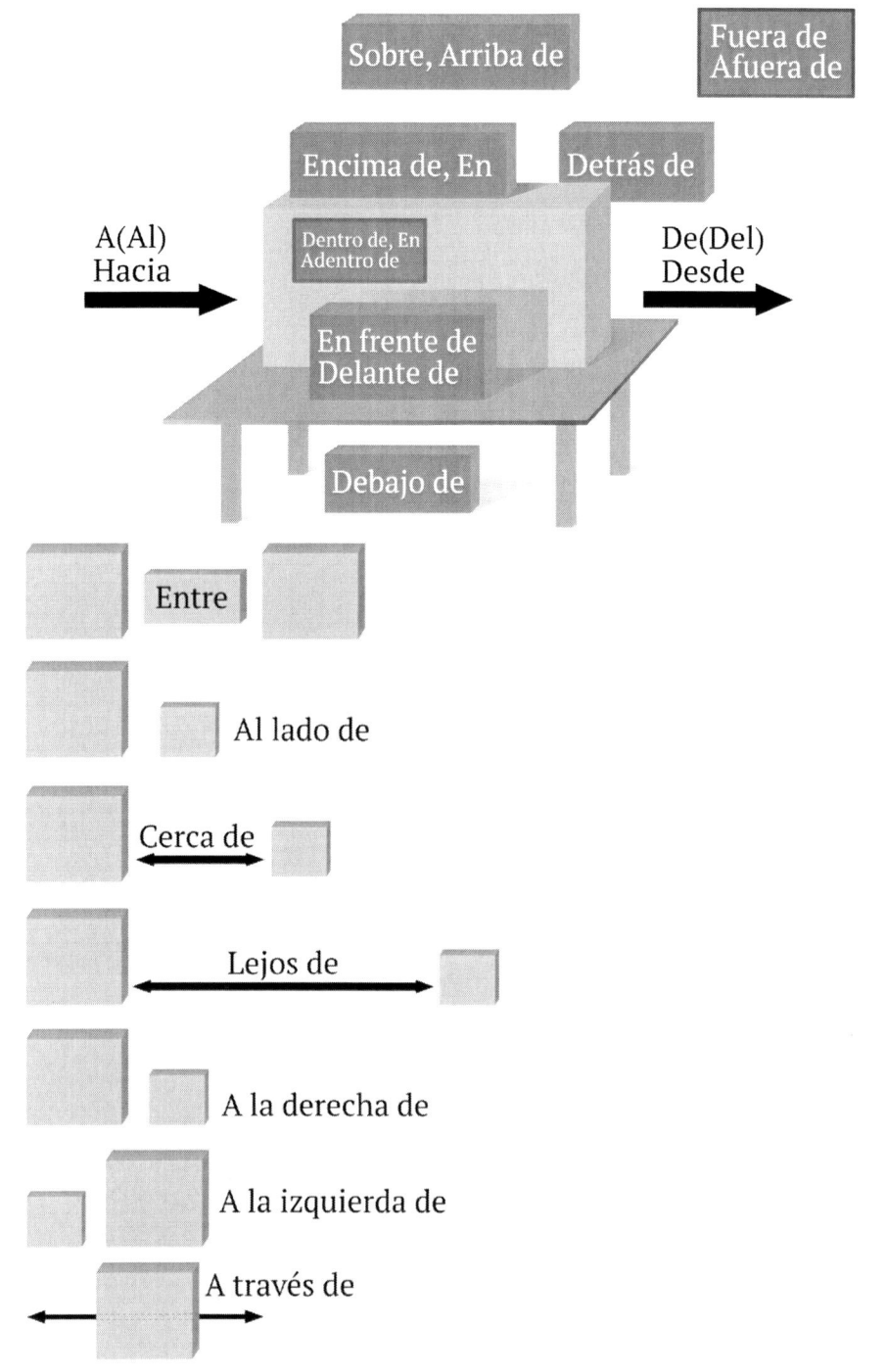

- Sobre, Arriba de
- Fuera de / Afuera de
- Encima de, En
- Detrás de
- A(Al) / Hacia
- Dentro de, En / Adentro de
- De(Del) / Desde
- En frente de / Delante de
- Debajo de
- Entre
- Al lado de
- Cerca de
- Lejos de
- A la derecha de
- A la izquierda de
- A través de

A, Al (a + el)	To
Hacia	Towards
De, Del(de + el)	From, of
Desde	Since, from
Dentro (de)	Inside, within
Adentro (de)	Inside, within
Interior	Inside (adjective)
En	In, on, at, into
Encima (de)	On, in top of
Sobre	Above, over, about
Arriba (de)	Above
Detrás (de)	Behind
En frente (de) Delante (de)	In front of (synonims)
Contra	Against
Debajo (de)	Under
Fuera (de)	Outside, out of
Afuera (de)	Ourside, out of
Entre	Between, among
Al lado de	Next to, at the side of, to the side of
Cerca (de)	Near, close to
Lejos (de)	Far
A través de	Through
Acerca de	About

Direction

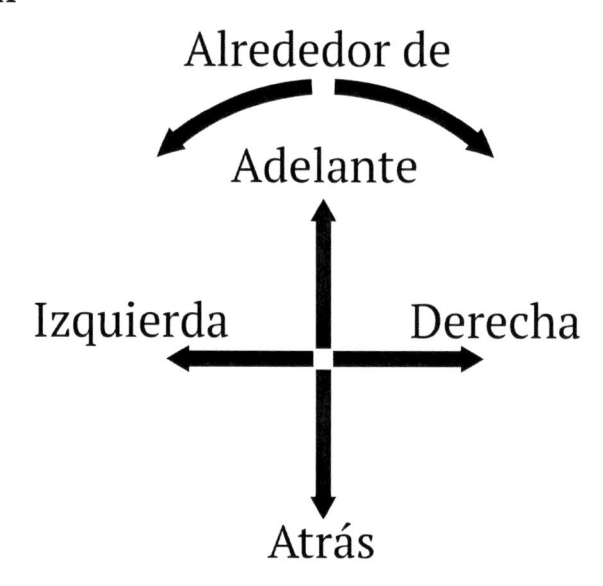

```
        Alrededor de
          ↙    ↘
         Adelante
            ↑
Izquierda ←—+—→ Derecha
            ↓
          Atrás
```

Alrededor (de)	Around
Adelante	Straight/ahead
Izquierda	Left
Derecha	Right
Atrás	Back

Time

Desde	Since	Durante	During
Antes de	Before	En	In (e.g. in one hour)
Ahora	Now	Mientras que	While
Despues de	After		
Hasta	Until/till		

There are nuances with some prepositions:

- **The preposition "a"** has far more ways of use than "to", you will see it in the next chapters.
- **Al, del** – this is simple: a + el = al, de + el = del.

Voy ~~a el~~ al teatro – I go to the theater

Ella habla ~~de el~~ del corazon – She speaks from the heart

- **De and desde:**

De has the meanings "from", "of", and desde has "from" and "since". Both of these prepositions can mean "from". When there is a **motion** in context, one can use **desde** as "from" equally to **de**:

Desde la República Dominicana viene el cacao = De la República Dominicana viene el cacao – Cacao comes from Dominican Republic

Venimos desde Australia = Venimos de Australia – We come from Australia

Also, *de* is used to describe a possession. In English we can describe possession with *of* or *'s*. In Spanish – with **de**.

La camisa de Daniela – Daniela's shirt

La casa de Gael – Gael's home

- **Dentro, adentro, en, interior:**

Dentro is usually used for emotional things:

Dentro de mi corazón – Inside of my heart

Dentro de tu alma – Inside of your soul

Adentro is usually used for physical things:

Adentro del edificio – Inside of the building

Adentro de la casa – Inside of the house

En means "in" or "on" or "at":

Las botellas están en la caja – The bottles are in the box

El archivo que Usted necesita está en mi computadora – The archive that you need is in my computer

Interior is not a preposition but adjective. It is placed in one line with prepositions for avoiding confusion:

Un detalle interior de su teléfono se rompió – An interior detail (a detail inside) of this phone got broken

La información interior – The inside information

- **Fuera and Afuera:** as well as DENTRO and ADENTRO:

Fuera is usually used for emotional things:

Fuera de tus abrazos – Out of of your hugs

Fuera de mis ilusiónes – Out of my illusions

Afuera is usually used for physical things:

Afuera de la pantalla – Out of the screen

Afuera del castillo – Outside of the castle

- **Encima de and En:**

Encima de means "on, in top of":

La cerveza está encima de la mesa – The beer is on the table

El nieve está encima del tejado – Snow is in top of the roof

- **Sobre and Acerca de.** SOBRE can mean either "Over"/"Above" or "About". ACERCA DE means "about":

Los pájaros vuelan sobre la ciudad – Birds fly above the city

¿Qué es eso sobre esa isla? – What is that above that island?

La rama del árbol está sobre mi cabeza – The branch of the tree is over my head

La maestra nos hablaba mucho sobre la historia de nuestro país – The teacher told us a lot about history of our country

¿Que sabemos sobre el día de hoy? – What do we know about today's date?

Él escribe acerca de animales salvajes – He writes about wild animals

La mayoría de las cancióneson acerca del amor – Majority of songs is about love

- **Alrededor de** means "Around", and also can mean "about" in meaning of amount:

Hay mucho gente inteligente alrededor de mí – There are a lot of smart people around me

Oigo muchos quejas alrededor de mí cada día – I hear many complaints around me every day

Filipe tiene alrededor de dos miles dolares – Filipe has about two thousand dollars

La distancía entre dos ciudades es alrededor de setecientos kilómetros – The distance between two cities is about seven hundred kilometers

Examples

Ella estará en casa después del trabajo – She will be at home after work

Él esperará al lado de la iglesia – He will wait next to the church

El auto estará en frente de la puerta – The car will be in front of the door

Dos naciones luchan una contra la otra – Two nations fight against each other

Vivo aquí por un tiempo largo, pienso que desde dos miles y uno – I have been living here for long time, I think that since 2001

Nuestros parientes nos visitan durante la semana de vacaciónes – Our relatives visit us during the vacational week

El tren va a París a través de Berlin – The train goes to Paris via Berlin

Pedro corrió hacia el autobús cuándo vió que las puertas se fue a cerrar – Pedro ran toward the bus when he saw that the doors were going to close

El policía se acercó a un hombre suspicaz y pidió mostrar qué estuvo adentro de su mochila – The policeman approached a suspicious man and asked him to show what was inside his backpack

Mi novia y yo vivimos lejos uno del otro – My girlfriend and I live far from each other

¿Qué vamos a hacer despues de la clase? – What are we going to do after the class?

Verbs that require a preposition

There are many verbs in the Spasnish language that must be accompanied with a preposition. You will find the list of these verbs in the additional content of this book in the chapter **"Verbs that require prepositions"**.

Examples

Yo aprendo a hablar Español – I learn to speak Spanish (aprender a)

Nosotros tratamos de estudiar – We try to study (tartar de)

Mi amigo se interesa por emprendimiento – My friend is interested in entrepreneurship (interesar por)

¿Puedes ayudarme a reparar la computadora? – Can you help me to repair the computer? (ayudar a)

¿Por que no confías en ella? – Why don't you trust her? (eonfiar en)

Javier acabó por trabajar en la agencia de mercadeo – Javier ended up working in marketing agency (acabar por)

Estos dulces saben a fresa – These sweets taste like strawberry (saber a)

Este té huele a un perfume – This tea smells like a perfume (oler a – to smell like)

A la mayoría de los chicos jóvenes les gusta jugar al fútbol – Most of young guys like to play football (jugar a)

El costo de la libertad es muy grande, hay que luchar por eso – The cost of freedom is very big, one must struggle for that (luchar por)

Yo no estaba por viajar a un cierto país pero cambió mi opinión – I was not in favor of traveling to a certain country but I changed my opinion

A tomar de juramento el presidente juró por la lealtad a la nación – By taking of the oath the president swore for the loyalty to the nation

Build sentences with these words:

la confianza – confidence	salvaje – wild	el garaje – garage
el diccionario – dictionary	rojo – red	el cuerpo – body
el destino – destination	la caja – box	el grupo – group
la promesa – promise	verde – green	el pueblo – village
el pájaro - bird	azul – blue	el estante – shelf

Exerises

Use appropriate preposition

1. Vendrán _____ dos horas – They will come in two hours
2. Voy a aparcar mi auto _____ este camion – I am going to park my car in the right of this truck
3. Son las seis _____ la mañana y no he dormido _____ toda la noche – It is 6 o'clock (of the morning) and I have not slept (during) the whole night
4. Me verás _____ la pared de ladrillo – You will see me in front of the brick wall
5. Hay la gente que trabaja _____ casa – There are people who work from home
6. Ustedes tienen que esperar _____ las siete – You have to wait until 7 o'clock
7. Al principio, debemos sacar las cajas _____ contenedor – At first, we must remove boxes from the container
8. Ponga el enlace _____ este sitio web en su página propia – Put the link to this website in your own page
9. Nadie vive en el piso _____ nuestro – No one lives in the floor above our
10. Hace frío _____ casa – It is cold outside of home
11. ¿Qué vas a hacer _____ terminar la Universidad? – What are you going to do after finishing university?
12. Ayer leí un artículo en un periódico _____ la segunda guerra mundial – Yesterday I read an article in a newspaper about the second world war
13. Lo costará _____ cien miles dolares – It will cost about one hundred thousand dollars
14. Él es _____ Estados Unidos – He is from United States
15. El gato duerme _____ mesa – The cat sleeps under the table
16. La cabeza está _____ cuerpo – The head is in top of the body

Answers

1: en, 2: a la derecha de, 3: de, durante, 4: en frente de/delante de, 5: desde, 6: hasta, 7: del/desde el 8: a, 9: arriba del, 10: afuera de, 11: después de, 12: sobre/acerca de, 13: alrededor de, 14: de, 15: debajo de la, 16: encima del

Lesson 8: Direct and indirect object Pronouns

In English there are pronouns "I, you, he, she, we, they", and there are pronouns "me, you, him, her, us, them". There are analogues in Spanish, however they are more complicated, because there are direct and indirect object pronouns, and pronouns with a preposition.

The table below shows the Spanish analogues of English pronouns "me, you, him, her, us, them".

Who?	Direct object	Indirect object	With preposition
Yo	me	me	mí
Tú	te	te	tí
Él	lo	le/se*	él
Ella	la	le/se*	ella
Usted	la	le/se*	usted
Nosotros(as)	nos	nos	nosotros(as)
Vosotros(as)	os	os	vosotros(as)
Ellos(as)	los(as)	les/se*	ellos(as)
Ustedes	los	les/se*	ustedes

*- *Le, Les placed before Lo, La, Los, Las become* **SE**

And the first question here is: what is the difference between direct and indirect object pronouns?

Direct object pronoun indicates an object of an action. Hint phrases are: "I can see (whom? What?)", "I use (whom? what?)" "I do (what?)"

Indirect object pronoun indicates an indirect object of an action. Hint phrases are: "I give (to whom? to what?)", "I do it (for whom? For what?)"

In English language the direct and indirect object pronouns match. However we can make some examples to show the difference between direct and indirect objects:

I give it to him – "it" is direct and "him" is indirect objects of the action "give" in this sentence.

43

We will send him to you – The action is "send", its direct object is "him", its indirect object is "you".

They do it for us – the action is "do", its direct object is "it", its indirect object is "us".

And in Spanish:

Ella lo ve – She sees him/it (direct)

Nosotros los necesitamos – We need them (direct)

Ellos nos explican – They explain to us (indirect)

Ustedes me prometieron – You promised me (indirect)

¿Por qué vosotros le prohibisteis? – Why did you prohibit him/her? (indirect)

Te recordaré siempre - I will remember you always (direct)

Analogue of English pronoun 'it':

The direct object pronouns pronouns LO and LA can be translated the following ways:

Lo – him, it;

La – her, it;

They all can mean "it", and it depends on grammatical gender of the object that we describe by this pronoun:

Yo compro el libro – I buy the book (el libro – masculine)

Yo lo compro – I buy it (it - masculine object)

Yo compro la comida – I buy food (la comida – feminine)

Yo la compro – I buy it (it - feminine object)

And as you can see, the pronouns Me, Te, Nos, Os match for direct and indirect objects.

When a sentence contains both direct and indirect objects, the indirect pronoun is always placed in front of the direct one:

Su jefe se lo dio – Her boss gave it to her (se – indirect, lo – direct)

No te lo dijimos – We didn't tell it to you (te – indirect, lo – direct)

¿Por qué no se lo ayudará? – Why it doesn't help me? (le – indirect, lo – direct)

It was already mentioned before that **le, les become SE in front of lo, los, la, las**, here are some more practical examples:

Nosotros ~~les~~ se lo damos – We give it to them

Por qué él no ~~le~~ se la da? – Why he doesn' give it to her?

Ella ~~le~~ se lo dio – She gave it to him

What's more: when we use a verb in infinitive, the pronoun (me, te, la, le, nos, os, los, las, les) is placed in the ending of a verb or in the beginning the sentence:

Ayudar – to help, Ayudar<u>nos</u> – to help us

No quiero preguntar<u>te</u> – I don't want to ask you

Te no quiero preguntar – I don't want tp ask you

Yo puedo explicar<u>te</u> – I can explain you

Te puedo explicar – I can explain you

¿Cuándo querías llamar<u>nos</u>? – When did you want to call us?

¿Cuándo nos querías llamar? – When did you want to call us?

And, an infinitive verb can be accompanied by both direct and indirect object pronouns at the same time. The following examples show equal expressions:

Quiero decír<u>telo</u> (<u>te</u> + <u>lo</u>) – I want to tell it to you

Te lo quiero decir – I want to tell it to you

Necesitamos comprar<u>selo</u> (<u>se</u> + <u>lo</u>) – We need to buy it for him/her/them. Don't forget that SE equals le/les when it is placed before lo, la, los, las.

Se lo necesitamos comprar – We need to buy it for him/her/them

¿Ustedes pueden dar<u>noslos</u>? (<u>nos</u> + <u>los</u>) – Can you give them to us?

¿Nos los pueden dar Ustedes? – can you give them to us?

Also, these pronouns can be used in the following ways:

- **Clarification and avoiding ambiguity**

As you could notice, the indirect object pronoun LE can have many meanings, i.e it can mean "him, her, it, you(formal)". That's why it can cause ambiguity, for example:

Le digo – I say him/her/it/you(formal)

Yo le di – I gave her/him/it/you(formal)

Ella se lo compra – She buys it for him/her/them/it/you(formal)

No se lo va a ayudar – It is not going to help him / her / them / it / you(formal)

Le escribo un mensaje – I write a message to him / her/ it / you(formal)

As you can see, there is ambiguity between "her, him, them, it, you(formal)" in such sentences in a context where the recipient of the action is not identified. If we want to clarify the object or person – receiver of the action, we have to add **A+OBJECT**:

Le digo a Pablo – I say it to Pablo

Yo le di a ella – I gave it to her

Ella se lo compra a su hermano – She buys it for her brother

No se lo va a ayudar a ellos – it is not going to help them

Le escribo un mensaje a mi madre – I write a message to my mother

- **Emphasis**

One can emphasize a recipient of an action by adding the same formula **A+OBJECT**:

Yo la veo – I see her

Yo la veo a ella, pero a los demás no – I see her, but not others. *(los demás - others)*. This expression emphasizes that I see exactly her but not anyone else

Nadie me da un consejo – Nobody gives me an advice

Nadie me da un consejo a mí* – Nobody gives me an advice, this expression emphasizes that nobody gives an advice exactly to me but not anyone else *(*- this is a pronoun with preposition)*

46

Pronouns with prepositions

And finally, we have one more category here - Personal pronouns **with preposition**. For example, with DE, A, POR, PARA, CON, EN and all others. All you need to memorize is only MÍ and TÍ, all others are the same as initial.

Examples

¿Por qué no quieres hacerlo conmigo? – Why don't you want to do it with me?

¿Qué hará ella con nosotros? – What will she do with us?

Quiero bailar contigo – I want to dance with you

Nadie puede cantar con ella – Nobody can sing with her

The personal "A"

When the direct object of an action is a **person** (animated object), we must use the preposition "A" before that. The personal "a" is used only when the direct object is a person:

Yo llamo a mi amiga – I call my friend. "Mi amiga" is the direct object of the action "yo llamo", and this is a person, so we must use the preposition "a" before it.

Nosotros vemos a nuestros padres – We see our parents. "Nosotros vemos" – action, "nuestros padres" – direct object as a person.

Ella ama a su gato – She loves her cat

¿A quien tú amas? – Who do you love?

Los padres apoyan a sus niños – The parents support their children

The rule A+el = Al is applied here too:

¿Tú viste al director? – Did you see the director?

Nosotros conocemos al autor de este libro – We know the author of this book

When the personal "a" is NOT used

- **When the direct object is not a person (inanimate object):**

Bebo la cerveza – I drink beer

Ella conduce un autobús – She drives a bus

- **With TENER – to have**:

Tengo muchos amigos – I have many friends

Tenemos una hermana – We have one sister

- **With HAY – there is:**

Hay cinco personas aquí – there are five persons here

Hay una chica que me gusta – there is one girl that I like

- **When the direct object is indefinite person:**

Ellos llaman un policía – They call a policeman

Él necesita nuevos empleos – He needs new employees

- **With animals that are not pets:**

Su hija vio un elefante en el zoo – His daughter saw an elephant in the zoo

¿Puedes atrapar ese pájaro? – Can you catch that bird?

Build sentences with these words:

la cosa – thing
el tejado – roof
la caja – box
el río – river
el lago – lake
el mar – sea
querido – dear,
rico – rich.
la leche – milk
el océano – ocean
el bosque – forest

el árbol – tree
el pescado – fish
la comida – food
el pan – bread,
le ensalada – salad
la carne – meat
el té – tea
el café – coffee
el vino – wine
la cerveza – beer
la tetera – teapot

el idioma – language,
el restaurante – restaurant,
el animal – animal
la naturaleza – nature
difícil – difficult
la cocina – kitchen
el camarero – waiter
el viajero – traveler
el puente – bridge
el castillo – castle
tranquilo - quiet

Exercises

Use appropriate pronoun (direct/indirect/with preposition)

1. Yo ___ prometo – I promise <u>her</u>
2. Dentro de ____ – Inside of <u>you</u>(tú)
3. ¿Ustedes ____ escuchan? – do you hear <u>us</u>?
4. ¿Qué quieres saber de ___ ? – What do you want to know from <u>me</u>?
5. El vendedor ____ dio lo que ellos quisieron – The seller gave <u>them</u> what they wanted
6. ¿Usted ____ ayudó? – Did you help <u>them</u>?
7. ¿____ permitiste? – Did you permit <u>him</u>?
8. Tu ___ ves? – Do you see <u>her</u>?
9. No quiero _____ (DECIR – to say/tell) – I don't want to tell you (tú)
10. ¿Quién ___ sabe? – who knows it?
11. ____ ayudaba a mi hermana muchos veces – I helped my sister many times
12. ____ dan mucho dinero a sus hijos – They give a lot of money to their children
13. Nosotros ____ ____ contamos – We told it to you(Usted)
14. Su padre se ____ dio a ella – Her father gave it to her
15. ¿Quién ____ ____ vendo? – Who sold it to you(tú)?
16. Recuerdas el mensaje que tú ____ enviaste _____? – Do you remember the message that you send <u>to her</u>?
17. Nuestro abuelo tiene un regalo para _____ - Our granddad has a gift for us
18. ¿Puedes cocinar algo para _____? – Can you cook something for me?
19. El maestro _____ dio las tareas a sus estudiantes – The teacher gave tasks to his students
20. Cómo tú ____ ____ explicaste _____? – How did you explain it to them?
21. Ella ____ quiere agradecer – She wants to thank <u>me</u>

Answers

1: le, **2:** tí, **3:** nos, **4:** mí, **5:** les, **6:** les, **7:** le, **8:** la, **9:** decirte, **10:** lo, **11:** le, **12:** les, **13:** se lo, **14:** lo/la, **15:** te lo, **16:** le, a ella, **17:** nosotros, **18:** mí, **19:** les, **20:** se los, a ellos, **21:** me

Lesson 9: More pronouns and important constructions

Possessive pronouns

Here is how to say "my, mine, your, yours etc.". These pronouns can be declined by gender and plural. Masculine gender has the ending –O, feminine – A, and plural has –S.

Mi – my, mío – mine

Tu – your, tuyo – yours

Su - his/her/its, your(for ustedes), suyo - his/her/its, your (for ustedes)

Nuestro(a) – our/ours

Vuestro(a) – our/ours

Su –their, suyo – theirs

As it was said before, these pronouns can be declined by gender and plural. Here are some examples:

Mi – my(singular), mis – my(plural)

Mío – mine(m), mía(f), mios(m, pl), mias(m, pl)

Tu, tus, tuyo(s), tuya(s)

Su, sus, suyo(s), suya(s)

Nuestro(s), nuestra(s)

Vuestro(s), vuestra(s)

Examples

La camiseta es mía – the T-shirt is mine

Nuestro pueblo – our village

Vuestras amigas – your friends (females)

Los bicicletas son suyas – the bicycles are theirs

Mi mujer es bonita – my wife is beautiful

Su hija es joven – his daughter is young

Ese bolso es suyo – this bag is hers

The pronoun "Lo"

LO is a special pronoun that can be used in some different ways.

- **First of all, as it was already considered before – as direct object pronoun "him/it":**

Yo lo hago – I do it

Nececitamos hacerlo – We need to do it

Él lo sabe – He knows it

¿Puedes comprenderlo? – Can you understand it?

- **As a neuter definite article:**

Lo bueno es que puedo hacerlo – The good thing is that I can do it

Lo mio es tuyo – What is mine is yours

Hacemos lo imposible – We do the impossible

- **Lo que – that, what:**

No todo lo que haces es correcto – Not everything that you do is correct

Pensaba que lo que él hace es bueno – I thought that what he does is good

Ellos memorizaron todo lo que estaba en la lección pero lo olvidaron pronto – They memorized everything that was in the lesson but they forgot soon

- **Sobre lo de – no direct translation, but the sense is close to "with regard to", "concerning", "in the matter of", "what about the":**

Sobre lo de mis estudios me parece bueno y no me es difícil – What about my studies is good and I don't have difficulties

Sobre lo de contrato, solo me queda firmarlo – Concerning the contract, I agree to sign it

Sobre lo de nuestro negocio, ahora todo está bien – What about our business, now everything is well

Idioms with Lo:

Por lo menos – at least

Por lo pronto – for now

Por lo general – generally

Por lo visto – apparently

Por lo tanto – therefore, thus, hence

A lo largo de – throughout

A lo mejor – at best

A lo lejos – in the distance

Examples

Lo que pasó entre ellos es muy triste – It is very sad what happened between them

Por lo menos yo no tengo que preocuparme – At least I don't have to worry

Lo bueno es que tú tienes este conocimiento – The good thing is that you have this knowledge

Lo importante es que este nicho es muy rentable – What's important is that this niche is very profitable

¿Dónde podemos encontrarlo? – Where can we find it?

Lo mejor es que ellos fueron advertido – The best thing is that they were warned

Todo lo que tú quieres de mí es muy estúpido – All that you want from me is very stupid

Lo increíble es que nos encontramos en un autobús por casualidad – The incredible thing is that we met each other in a bus accidentally

Por lo visto a Simona no le interesa nuestra oferta – Apparently Simona is not interested in our offer

Something, everywhere, nobody etc.

Person:

Alguien – somebody
Todos – everybody
Nadie – nobody

Thing:

Algo – something
Todo – everything
Nada – nothing

Time:

A veces – sometimes
Siempre – always
Jamas/Nunca – never

Place:

(En) alguna parte – somewhere
(En) todas partes – everywhere
(En) ninguna parte – nowhere

Double negation is possible in Spanish. If in English we should say "he didn't say anything" instead of "he didn't say nothing", in Spanish we can say so:

Él <u>no</u> dijo <u>nada</u> - He said nothing

<u>No</u> lo hicimos <u>nunca</u> – We never did it

<u>Nadie</u> hizo <u>nada</u> – Nobody did anything

Examples

Jorge fumaba a veces – Jorge smoked sometimes

Yo y mis amigos viajamos a alguna parte cada año – I and my friends travel somewhere every year

No queremos nada ahora – We don't want anything now

Notice, that in Spanish one can use two negations at the same time: "no queremos nada" instead of "queremos nada".

Él estudiaba todas las noches – he studied every night

El viajero quiere ir a todos partes – The traveler wants to go everywhere

Nunca intenté fumar – I never tried to smoke

Nadie jamas envió el reporte – Nobody ever sent a report

This, that, these, those

These pronoun are known as "demonstratives".

Este (m), esta (f) – This

Estos (m, pl), estas (f, pl) – These

Ese (m), esa (f, pl) – That

Esos (m, pl), esas (f, pl) – Those

Aquel (m), aquella (f) – that (over there)

Aquellos (m, pl), aquellas (f, pl) – those (over there)

Also, there are neuter demonstratives that don't change gender and number, they refer to an unknown thing or emotion:

Esto – this

Eso – that

Aquello – that (over there)

Examples

Aquella montaña está lejos de acá – That mountain (over there) is far from here

Este libro es muy interesante – This book is very interesting

Esto es bueno – This is good

¿Qué es eso? – What is that?

Estas playas son hermosas – These beaches are beautiful

¿Dónde está este castillo? – Where is this castle?

Aquellas islas están cerca de la costa – Those islands are close from the coast

Here and there

Aquí – here, the closest distance from the speaker, for example "here, on my table", "here, in this cupboard"

Acá – here, more generalized meaning, for example or "here, in Madrid" or "here, in Argentina"

Ahí – there, minimal distance for example "there, on the shelve"

Allí – there, medium distance that you cannot point out, for example "over there, in that hill"

Allá – there, farther distance, that you cannot point out, for example "there, in the central park"

Examples

Lo pondré aquí – I will put it here

No sé qué es eso allí – I don't know what it is there

Nosotros estuvimos allá - We have been there

Acá tenemos elecciones presidenciales cada cuatro años – We have the president elections every 4 years here.

¿Cuándo usted fue para allá? – When you went there?

La tetera está ahí, en la cocina – The teapot is there, in the kitchen

Unos viajeros estaban allá, como él me dijo – Some travelers were there, as he told me

¿Dondé está el restaurante acá? – Where is the restaurant here?

Pero esa calle está allí – But that street is there

¿Por cierto, puedes buscarlo allá? – By the way, can you search it there? (medium distance)

¿Qué occurrió allá en la playa ayer? – What happened there in the square yesterday?

¿Qué buscas ahí? – What are you searching there?

¿Oyes la música allí? – do you hear the music there?

¿Qué vosotros comisteís allá? – Which food did you eat there?

Exercises

Use appropriate locative pronoun (here, there)

1. ¿Cuando tú visitaste Perú, qué viste _____ ? – When you visited Peru, what did you see <u>there</u>?
2. ¿Por qué lo pusiste _____ ? – Why did you put it <u>here</u>?
3. ¿Quién estuvo _____ antes de mí? – Why has been <u>here</u> before me?
4. ¿Se puede enviar la carta _____ , yo significo, a Inglaterra? – Can one send the letter <u>there</u>, I mean, to England?
5. ¿Sabes que tenemos mucho cosas _____ ? – You know it, that we have much stuff <u>here</u> (closest distance)?
6. No lo vi _____ porque estuve ocupado – I didn't see it <u>there</u> because I was busy
7. ¿A quién vas a encontrar _____? – Whom are you going to meet <u>here</u>?
8. El mensajero entregará el paquete _____ – The courier will deliver the parcel <u>there</u>
9. Nadie sabe que puedo encontrar _____ en mi habitación – Nobody knows what I can find here in my room

Use appropriate demonstrative pronoun (this, that)

10. ¿Qué es _____ en el tejado? – What is <u>that</u> on the roof?
11. ¿Por qué me trajiste _____ cajas? – Why did you bring me <u>these</u> boxes?
12. No quiero ir a_____ lugar – I don't wanna go to <u>that</u> place
13. _____ es tan bello! – <u>This</u> is so beautiful!
14. _____ consejo fue muy mal – This advice was very bad
15. Por favor, compra _____ cosas en la tienda – Please, buy <u>these</u> things in the store
16. Las mujeres no aman _____ perfume – Women don't like <u>this</u> perfume
17. Nadie sabe qué es _____ – Nobody knows what is <u>that</u>
18. ¿Llegó Usted a un acuerdo con _____ gerente? – Did you reach an agreement with <u>this</u> manager?

Answers

1: allá, **2**: aquí, **3**: acá, **4**: allá, **5**: aquí, **6**: allá, **7**: aquí, **8**: allá, **9**: aquí **10**: aquello, **11**: estas, **12**: ese, **13**: esto, **14**: este, **15**: estas, **16**: este **17**: eso, **18**: este

Lesson 10: Important words and constructions

Pero	but	Ni … ni	neither … nor
También	too	O … o	either … or
Porque	because	Tal	such
A causa de	because of	Tan	so, such
Debido a	due to	Así	so, thus
Entonces	then	Por lo tanto	therefore
Demasiado	too (much)	Además	also, moreover
Tanto	so much	Por otro lado	on the other hand
Sólo	only	El/la/lo mismo	the same
Así que	as well as	Tan … como	as … as
A pesar de	despite of	En lugar de	instead of
Tampoco	neither	Aun	even
Quizas	Perhaps/maybe	Aún	yet, still
Tal vez	Maybe	Aunque	although/even if
Más	more	Ya	already, anymore
Aparte de	apart from	Todavía	still, yet
Con	with	Incluso	even
Cada	Each/every	Bastante	quite
A pesar de	despite	Sin	without
De nuevo	again	Ni siquiera	not even
A través de	through	Mientras que	while
Cualquier	any	Sin embargo	however
Al contrario	In contrary	A diferente de	unlike
Más bien	rather	El uno al otro	each other
Hace …	… ago		

Examples:

No puedo hacerlo sin tí, puedo sólo contigo – I can't do it without you, I can only (do it) with you

Hay demasiado hongos en ese bosque – There are a lot of mushrooms in that forest

En lugar de ir al teatro, Juan fui al cine – Instead of going to the theater, Juan went to the cinema

A pesar de estar enfermo, el deportista participó en la competencia – Despite of being ill, the sportsman participated in the competition

No quiero ni jugar ni dormir y ni siquiera comer – I don't want neither to play nor to sleep or even eat

¿Usted no cree que es posible a beber dos botellas de vodka en seguida? Yo tampoco – You don't believe that it is possible to drink two bottles of vodka at once? Neither do I

Lo hicimos hace cinco años – We did it five years ago

La música fue bastante rudiosa, aunque no nos molestó – The music was quite loud although it didn't disturb us

Mientras que estuvieron en la playa nosotros cocinamos la comida para ustedes – While you were in the beach we cooked food for you

Maria viajaba en autobús cada día pero hoy decidió caminar todo el camino – Maria traveled by bus every day but today decided to walk the whole way

Levante la mano y entonces pregunte que Usted quiere – Raise your hand and then ask what you want

Lo siento, llegué tarde a causa de embotellamiento – I am sorry, I was late because of traffic jam

¿Sigues trabajando, o ya has terminado? – Are you still working or have already finished?

Lo debes completar en cualquier manera – You must complete it in any way

El programador todavía está atrapado con una tarea dificíl – The programmer in stuck with a difficult task

Todavía, Incluso, Aún, Aun

These words mean either "still/yet or even" and can confuse at first sight. Let's figure out when an where to use each of them:

- **Todavía – still/yet**.

Perdóname si me amas todavía – Forgive me if you still love me

¿Ese sitio web todavía existe? – Does that website still exist?

¿Por qué razón Jorge no ha sido promovido todavía? – For what reason Jorge has not still been promoted?

- **Incluso - even**

Papá Noel trajo los regalos no solo para niños pero incluso para su padres – Santa Claus brought gifts not only for kids but even for their parents

Incluso sin tener la educación superior él gana mucho – Even without having high education he earns a lot

Antonio quiere comer siempre, incluso justo después de la cena – Antonio always wants to eat, even just after dinner

- **Aún (wtih stress mark):** equals *Todavía* in meaning of time, and equals *Incluso* in phrase like "even more, even better", i.e. with any comparative word.

Ella sabe aún más que yo – She knows even more than me

Juan es aún más complicado que ella – Juan is even more complicated than she

Es mejor aún de lo que esperaba – It is even better than I expected

Su pizza aún no está preparada – Your (formal) pizza is not ready yet

Aún me duele la cabeza – I still have headache

El tren aún no ha llegado – The train has still not come

- **Aun (without stress mark)** equals *Incluso*. Also, always used before gerunds (i.e. present tense participle ending in –ando/-iendo) instead of *Inclus*.

Aun así, no reacciona – Even so, it doesn't react

Aun estudiando, no apruebo – Even studying, I don't approve

Aun pagando por cursos caros, no gasta mucho – Even paying for expensive courses, he doesn't spend much.

Use of Mismo

The word "Mismo" can be either pronoun or adjective or adverb.

- **El mismo/La misma – The same**

¿Por qué todos leen los mismos libros en el colegio? – Why do everyone read the same books in the college?

Dos gemelos llevan las mismas camisetas – Two twins wear the same T-shirts

Su método de estudiar idiomas es el mismo – His method of studying languages is the same

- **Lo mismo – check the chapter "The pronoun lo" in the previous lesson**, where "lo as a neuter definitive article". In this case "lo" is exactly this thing. So, "Lo mismo" actually means "what is the same/ that which is the same/ the same thing"

Él no va a decir nada nuevo, sólo todo lo mismo – He is not going to say anything new, only the same things

- **Mí mismo – myself, Ti mismo – yourself, Sí mismo – himself/herself/themselves/oneself**

¿Puedes hacerlo port ti mismo? – Can you do it by yourself?

Miranda aprendió a tocar guitarra por sí mismo – Miranda learned to play guitar by herself

Lo puedo reparar por mi mismo – I can repair it by myself

- **Ahora mismo – right now, Aquí mismo – right here and other constructions like these with "right".**

Le llamaré ahora mismo – I will call him right now

Les esperaremos ahí mismo – We will wait you right there

Ella encontró su billetera perdida aquí mismo – She found her lost wallet right here

Exercises

A. Use either AÚN or AUN or INCLUSO or TODAVÍA

1. Esta pantalla es _____ más grande que la que vimos antes – This screen is even bigger than that one that we saw before
2. Esta calle es _____ más rudioso – This street is even more loud
3. _____ dejando la casa por un tiempo largo, él estaba feliz – Even leaving home for long time, he was happy
4. La sopa _____ está caliente – The soup is still hot
5. Es muy bien que _____ tu abuelo viejo vino a visitarme en mi cumpleaños – It is very good that even your old grandad came to visit me in my birthday
6. La lluvia _____ penetra tejado – Rain still penetrates our roof
7. Sin duda, tu vestido nuevo es _____ más bello que lo que vestiste ayer – Without doubt, your new dress is even more beautiful than that one that you wore yesterday

B. Use MISMO with appropriate article in appropriate form

8. Probablemente ya recibíeron _____ preguntas muchas veces – Probably they already received the same questions many times
9. Tal vez deberíamos tratar de hacer _____ - Maybe we should try to do the same?
10. _____ ideas dirigen a la competencia a veces – The same ideas lead to competition sometimes
11. En el año pasado nada se cambió, todo es _____ - Nothing got changed in the previous year, everything is the same
12. Están cansados de _____ cosas cada día – They are tired of the same things every day

Answers

1: aún/incluso, 2: aún/incluso, 3: aun, 4: aún/todavía, 5: aun/incluso, 6: aún/todavía, 7: aún/incluso, 8: las mismas, 9: lo mismo, 10: las mismas, 11: lo mismo, 12: las mismas

Lesson 11: Por/Para and reflexive verbs

Por and *para*

There are two conjunctions: Por and Para, both of which have the meaning "for", and other meanings. And this subject can be complicated.

When to use PARA:

- **PARA as "for" in sentences kind of "Something for something", i.e. for recipient**

Lo hago para tí – I do it for you

Este bar es bueno para la fiesta – This bar is good for the party

Él regaló las flores para su novia – He gave the flowers for his girlfriend

- **PARA as "In order to, to" / "for doing something" / "for the purpose of", i.e. for goals**

Ahorramos el dinero para viajar – We save money in order to travel/ for traveling

Él invierte el dinero en criptomonedas para lucrar – He invests money to crypto-currencies in order to profit

Ella estudia duro para obtener la educación – She studies hard to get an education

- **Indication of destination, e.g. IR PARA – to go to**

*In this case **IR PARA** equals **IR A***

Ella va para Nueva-York = Ella va a Nueva-York – She goes to New-York

Hoy voy a ir para la fiesta = Hoy voy a ir a la fiesta – Today I am going to go to the party

¿Cuándo volverás para Bolivia? = ¿Cuándo volverás a Bolivia? – When you return to Bolivia?

- **PARA as BY,ON in the sentences like "by Monday, on Tuesday etc.", i.e for deadlines**

Tengo que estar aquí para el martes – I have to be here by the Tuesday

¿Qué vas a hacer para el lunes? – What are you going to do on Monday?

La computadora debe estar disponible para las ocho – The computer must be available at eight o'clock

When to use POR:

- **POR as analogue of English "for" in meaning of duration**

Mi amigo de Brasil llegó a mi casa por una semana – My friend from Brasil came to my home for one week

Estaremos aquí por dos días – We will be here for two days

La moneda de nuestro país estaba creciendo por un largo tiempo – The currency of our country was growing for long time

- **POR as "via, through"**

Yo voy a Amsterdam por Berlin – I go to Amsterdam via Berlina

Viajaremos a los Caribes por Madrid – We will travel to the Caribbeans via Madrid

Tenemos que caminar por un barrio peligroso cada día – We have to walk through a dangerous district everyday

- **POR as BY in sentences kind of "do something by something", "travel by (vehicle)"**

Prefiero hablar sobre eso por teléfono – I prefer to talk about that by phone

Te gusta viajar por tren? – Do you like to travel by train?

Ella corta la ensalada por un cuchillo – She slices the salad by knife

- **POR as English "per", e.g. "per hour"**

Cien kilómetros por hora – Hundred kilometers per hour (100km/h)

La fábrica puede producir cincuenta automóviles por día – The factory can produce fifty automobiles per day

¿Cuántos páginas puedes leer por un minuto? – How many pages can you read for one minute?

- **Thanking for, respect for, love for**

Te agradezco mucho por tu regalo – I tank you a lot for your gift

Ellos tienen mucho respeto por nuestra nación – They have a lot of respect for our nation

Ella siente mucho amor por todo lo que hace – She feels much love for everything that she does

- **When one trades, exchanges one thing for another**

Le pagué diez dolares por la ayuda – I payed him ten dollars for the help

Vamos a intercambiar nuestros dolares por los pesos mexicanos – Let's exchange our dollars for Mexican pesos

¿Cuanto pacas por los clases de baile? – How much do you pay for dance classes?

- **POR as FOR in meaning of "on behalf of"**

El ingeniero trabaja por una empresa tecnológica – The engineer works for a technological enterprise (on behalf of a technological company)

Lo hago por su solicitud – I do it for his request (on behalf of his request)

Confiamos en su apoyo por este proyecto – We rely on their support for this project (on behalf of this project)

- **Reasoning, like "because of …", "for …"**

Port tí yo cambié mi vida – Because of you I changed my life

Por su idea, Daniel tiene que trabajar duro – Because of his idea, Daniel has to work hard

Helena trabaja como voluntaria en un hospital por su deseo de ayudar a la gente – Helena works as a volunteer in a hospital because of her wish to help people

- **In the morning, afternoon, at night**

Por la mañana – In the morning
Por la tarde – In the afternoon
Por la noche – At night

Te llamaré por la mañana – I will call you at morning

¿Ad ónde vamos a ir por la noche? – Where are we going to go at night?

A los niños les gusta dormir por la tarde – The kids like to sleep in the afternoon

- **With verbs that require the prepositions POR**

You will find these verbs in the chapter "Verbs that require prepositions"

Idioms with POR and PARA:

Por ejemplo – for example

Por cierto – By the way

Por tu culpa – Because of you

Por supuesto – of course

Por fin – finally

Para siempre – forever

Para que – so that

Examples

Esto es un regalo para tí – This is a gift for you

No quiero estudiarlo para trabajar allí – I don't want to study it in order to work there

Él lo estudia para ser especialista – He studies it for the purpose of being a specialist

Voy para tomar una cerveza más – I am going to take one more beer

Yo deje de fumar por tu culpa – I gave up smoking because of you

Por fin podemos descansar de eso – Finally we can relax form that

Reflexive verbs and reflexive pronouns

A reflexive verb is a verb that refer to a reflexive action, or simply to say, an action that a subject performs on itself. Or, one can explain it as so: the subject of the action and receiver of the action are the same.

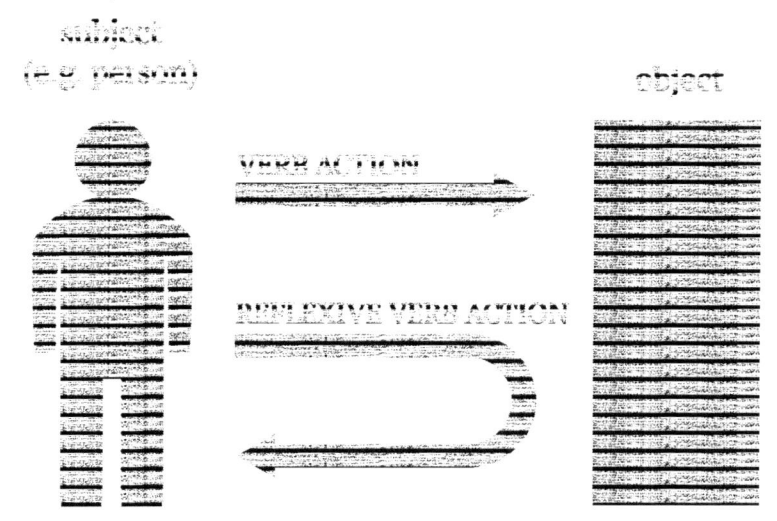

Reflexive verbs have the postfix –SE after ending in the infinitive form. Any verb can be reflexive. Conjugation of these verbs is the same as of non-reflexive verbs, but they are accompanied by reflexive pronouns:

Pronoun	Reflexive pronoun	
Yo	me	myself
Tú	te	yourself
Él, ella, usted	se	oneself, himself, herself
Nosotros	nos	ourselves
Vosotros	os	yourselves
Ellos, ustedes	se	themselves, yourselves

Llamarse – to call oneself

Me llamo	I call myself
Te llamas	You call yourself
Se llama	He, she calls himself

Nos llamamos	We call ourselves
Os llamáis	You call yourselves
Se llaman	They call themselves

By the way, the expression ME LLAMO also means "My name is" (literal meaning is "I call myself).

- **Some reflexive verbs can be translated to English as "to do something with oneself", for example:**

Cubrir – to cover

Cubrirse – to cover oneself

- **Some reflexive verbs are equivalent of English reflexive construction "to get …", for example:**

Vestir – to dress,

Vestir*se* - to get dressed.

In English, in this case the word "get" indicates reflexion.

- **And some reflexive verbs have own translation:**

Preocuparse – to worry, Irse – to leave (formed from IR), Ponerse – to put on, Quedarse – to stay, Acostarse – go to bed.

- **Here is how to use reflexive verbs in practice:**

Ella se viste rápidamente – She gets dressed quickly

Me sentí enfermo ayer – I felt (myself) sick yesterday

No nos preocuparemos – We will not worry

- **When a reflexive verb is used with a modal verb**, i.e. with QUERER, TENER QUE, DEBER, NECESITAR, PODER, one can place a reflexive pronoun after the infinitive form of a reflexive verb, or before a verb. Here are two examples:

Tengo que duchar*me* antes de salir = *Me* tengo que duchar antes de salir – I have to take a shower before leaving

Quiero despertar*me* temprano = *Me* quiero despertar temprano – I want to wake up early

Conjugate these reflexive verbs with all pronouns and build sentences with them:

llamar*se* – to call oneself
ir*se* – to leave (formed from ir)
encontrar*se* – to meet
reunir*se* – to get together
poner*se* – to put on
casar*se* – to get married
preocupar*se* – to worry
quedar*se* – to stay
duchar*se* – to take shower

despertar*se* – to wake up
lavar*se* – to get washed
levantar*se* – to get up
sentir*se* – to feel oneself
vestir*se* – to get dressed
acostar*se* – go to bed
volver*se* – to become
acostumbrar*se* – to get used to
emborrachar*se* – to get drunk

Examples

Sofía y Santiago se casaron hace dos años – Sofia and Santiago got married two years ago

Me acostumbré a ir por este camino – I got used to go by this path

Debemos acercarnos a nuestro objetivo cada día paso a paso – We must get closer to our aim everyday step by step

Quiero reunirme con mis amigos en el evento – I want to get together with my friends in the event

¿Cuándo nos tenemos que acostar? – When we have to go to bed?

Su habitación se volvió hermosa despues de reparación – Her room became beautiful after repair

Esta lavadora se rompará pronto – This washing machine will get broken soon

Debemos quedarnos aquí hasta mañana – We must stay here until tomorrow

Ellos están seguros que nunca se equivocan – They are sure that they are never mistaken

Mi hermana se casa con mi amigo – My sister gets married with my friend

¡Cuando el Bitcoin estuvo barato, no nos damos cuenta que lo puede subir un cohete! – When the Bitcoin was cheap, we didn't realize that it can skyrocket!

Exercises

Conjugate reflexive verbs

1. ¿Por qué _____ tanto? (PREOCUPARSE – to worry) – Why do you(vosotros) worry too much?
2. ¡Quiero _____ con la cobija! (CUBRIRSE – to cover oneself) – I want to cover myself by the blanket!
3. Esta computadora no _____ (REPARARSE –to get repaired) – This computer doesn't get repaired (One doesn't repair this computer)
4. Mi teléfono _____ por una hora (CARGARSE – to get charged) – My phone gets charged for one hour
5. Pienso que tengo que _____ ahora (IRSE – to leave) – I think that I have to leave now
6. Su madre _____ cuando ella soltó la copa (ENOJARSE – to get angry) – Her mother got angry when she dropped the glass
7. ¿Cuando ustedes _____ ? (CASARSE – to get married) – When you get married?
8. ¿Cómo _____ usted hoy? (SENTIRSE – to feel oneself) – How do you you feel (yourself) today?
9. Ella y su compañero _____ para un viaje (PREPARAR – to get prepared) – She and her companion get prepared for a trip
10. Ayer por la noche _____ en la calle (ENCONTRARSE – to meet) – We met in the street at night yesterday
11. _____ en esta silla (SENTARSE – to sit) – You can sit on this chair
12. _____ temprano cada día (DESPERTARSE – to wake up) – We wake up early everyday
13. ¿Cómo _____ ? (SENTIRSE – to feel) –How do you(tú) feel?
14. ¿Por qué Ustedes no _____? (ACOSTARSE – to go to bed) – Why you don't go to bed?
15. No puedo _____ (DORMIRSE – to fall asleep) – I can't fall asleep

Answers

1: os preocupáis, **2**: cubrirme, **3**: se repara, **4**: se carga, **5**: irme, **6**: se enoja, **7**: se casan, **8**: se siente, **9**: se preparan, **10**: nos encontrábamos, **11**: te puedes sentar, **12**: nos despertamos **13**: te sientes, **14**: se acuestan, **15**: dormirme

Lesson 12: Verbs like "GUSTAR" and Passive voice

There are verbs like GUSTAR, IMPORTAR, ENCANTAR and others and they look like usual verbs. However, there is a trick with these verbs – these verbs have reflexive sense.

Let's consider the verb **GUSTAR** – to like, or literally, it means "to be liked".

In English we say: "I like it", but in Spanish we literally say "it is pleased to me/it pleases me" – ME GUSTA, i.e. literally subject and object swap places. With verbs like this we have to use indirect object pronouns: ME, TE, LE, NOS, OS, LES.

These verb are conjugated like any other verbs: yo gusto, tú gustas, él gusta, nosotros gustamos, vosotros gustáis, ellos gustan. However, they are never used this way.

YO GUSTO doesn't mean "I like", it means "I am pleased to myself". But ME GUSTA means "I like", or literally "It is pleased to me".

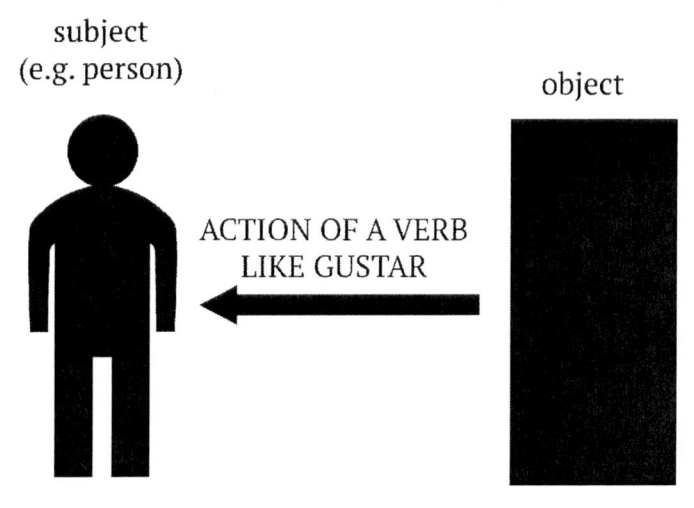

Look at more examples with GUSTAR:

Te gusta – you like (is pleased to you)

Nos gusta – we like (is pleased to us)

Le gusta – he/she likes (is pleased to he/she)

Nosotros te gustamos – you like us (we are pleased to you)

Usted le gusta – You like her/him (he/she is pleased to you)

¿Ella me gusta? – Does she like me? (am I pleased to her?)

Les gustan los melocotónes – They like peaches (peaches are pleased to them)

Also, in order to clarify a pronoun, one can use the construction: **A + prepositional pronoun** (lesson 8) before such verb:

A mí me gusta – I like

A tí te gusta – You like

A él le gusta – He likes

A nosotros nos gusta – We like

A Emma le gusta – Emma likes

Al jefe le gusta – The boss likes

And so on.

The verbs like GUSTAR just should be memorized. There is not a rule on how to detect them. Build sentences with these verbs of this type:

Doler – to be painful to	Molestar – to be bothering to
Aburrir – to bore	Bastar – to be sufficient
Caer bien – to suit	Disgustar – to be disgusted to
Caer mal – to not suit	Quedar – to be left over/to remain
Agradar – to be pleased by	Volver loco – to be crazy about
Fascinar – to be fascinated to	Faltar – to be lacking something
Encantar – to be delighted	Interesar – to be interested in
Importar – to be important to	Parecer – to appear to be

Examples

Le interesa la informática – He is interested in IT

A él le gusta la informática – He is interested in IT

¿Por qué a ustedes no les gusta bailar? – Why don't you like to dance?

¿A dónde a ella le encanta viajar? – Whereto does she love to travel?

¡No me importa que ellos piensen eso de mí! – I don't care (it is not important to me) that they think so about me!

A los turistas les gustan los museos – The tourists like the museums

¿A quién le gusta bailar salsa? – Who likes to dance salsa?

No me faltan ni la motivación ni la productividad – I don't have lack of motivation and productivity (literally: neither motivation nor productivity)

A esa gente no lo importa nada – Those people don't care about anything/For those people nothing is important

Esta música les aburrió a todos – This music bored everybody

Les agradan las actividades al aire libre – They are pleased by outdoor activities

Ahora solo le queda pagar las cuentas – Now he just has to pay the bills (literally: Now the bills just remain to be paid by him)

A la mayoría de los chicos jóvenes les gusta jugar al fútbol – Most of young guys like to play football

Passive voice

In English, we can say "one says, one does, one makes", or "we are told, it is said, I am told" etc. In the Spanish language, we can say so with help of the pronoun SE.

And a verb accompanied with the pronoun SE will be conjugated as with the pronoun él/ella/Usted, or s with ellos/ellas/Ustedes in plural form.

Se habla – one says

Se puede – one can

Se permite – one permits

Las idiomas extranjeros se estudian mucho – The foreign languages are studied a lot

"It is"

In order to say "it is" in Spanish, just use SER or ESTAR conjugated with Él/Ella/Usted – ES or ESTÁ:

Es bien que lo amas – It is good that you love it

Ya es tarde – It is late already

Está lluvioso – It is rainy

Weather idioms

There are weather idioms that are formed with the verb HACER. This verb is conjugated with Él/Ella/Usted. These expressions should just be memorized:

Hace frío – it is cold

Hace calor – it is hot

Hace sol – it is sunny

Have viente – it is windy

Hace buen/mal tiempo – The weather is good/bad

Examples

Se dice que no podemos entrar allí – One says that we can't come in there

Se leen los libros en esta biblioteca desde las ocho hasta las nieve de la tarde – In this library the books are read from eight o'clock until nine o'clock of the evening.

Los castillos de nuestro país se exploran mucho – The castles of our country are explored a lot

¿Qué se dijo en ese discurso? – What was said in that speech?

La cámara se usa a menudo – The camera is used often

¿Cómo se dice en ruso? – How it is said in Russian?

Se vende el apartamento por treinta miles dolares – One sells the apartment for thirty thousands dollars

Se parece que perdemos mucho tiempo aquí – It seems that we lost a lot of time here

Se juega el fútbol en este campo – One plays football in this field

Exercises

Conjugate verbs of this type

1. La torre en esta ciudad _____ muchos turistas (Gustar – to like) – Many tourists like the tower in this city
2. _____ agua (FALTAR – to be lacking) – I lack the water
3. Los verbos de segunda y tercera conjugación _____ igual que en el pretérito imperfecto (CONJUGAR – to conjugate) – The verbs from 1st and 2nd conjugations are conjugated the same in the imperfect preterite.
4. Yo voy a un banco y entonces_____hacer compras en una tienda (GUSTAR – to like) – I go to a bank and then I would like to do shopping in a store
5. No _____ los juegos de computadora, ni la televisión (INTERESAR – to be interested in) – They were interested neither in computer games nor in television
6. A nosotros_____los conocimientos para la próxima clase (FALTAR – to be lacking) – We are lacking the knowledges for the next class
7. _____ estas palabras una y otra vez (REPETIR – to repeat) – One repeats these words again and again
8. Tú_____(GUSTAR – to like) – I like you
9. Por lo visto, _____ esta parte muy rápido (CAMBIAR – to change) – Apparently, one changes this part very quickly
10. Pienso que yo _____ a ella (GUSTAR – to like) – I think that she likes me
11. Me _____ su hospitalidad ayer (AGRADAR – to please) – I was pleased by his hospitality yesterday
12. ¿Qué más _____ hacer en este trabajo? (QUEDAR – to left over/to remain) – What else remains to be done in this job?
13. Mi madre me regaló una cosa que _____ mucho (ENCANTAR – to be delighted to) – My mother presented me one thing that I loved a lot

Answers

1: les gusta a, **2**: me falta, **3**: se conjugan, **4**: me gustaría, **5**: les interesan, **6**: nos faltan, **7**: se repiten, **8**: me gustas, **9**: se cambia, **10**: le gusto, **11**: agradó, **12**: te queda **13**: me encantó

Lesson 13: Conditional mood and degrees of comparison

In English the conditional mood is formed by the word "would", e.g. "I would do, I would speak", but in Spanish it is formed by endings.

There is not difference between –AR, -ER, -IR verbs in the conditional mood. All verbs, including irregular ones, have stems the same as in the future tense.

Olvidar – to forget

Yo olvidaría	I would forget
Tú olvidarías	You would forget
Él, ella, usted olvidaría	He, she, You would forget
Nosotros olvidaríamos	We would forget
Vosotros olvidaríais	You would forget
Ellos, ustedes olvidarían	They, You would forget

Example of an irregular verb, as it was said before – the stem is the same as in future tense.

Poner – to put. In the future tense this verb is irregular and has the stem PONDR-

Yo pondría	I would put
Tú pondrías	You would put
Él, ella, usted pondría	He, she, You would put
Nosotros podríamos	We would put
Vosotros podríais	You would put
Ellos, ustedes podrían	They, You would put

Conjugate these verbs in conditional mood with all pronouns:

Incluir – to include
Pagar – to pay (for)
Aceptar – to accept
Emplear – to employ

Correr – to run
Servir – to serve
Perder – to lose
Sufrir – to suffer

Asegurarse – to make sure,
Acordarse – to remember,
Reconocer – recognize,
Participar – to participate,

Examples

¿Memorizarías el poema? – would you memorize the poem?

¿Dibujaría algunas illustraciónes para mi libro? – would you(usted) write some illustrations for my book?

¿Cómo lo dirías en inglés? – how would you say that in English?

Yo compraría un nuevo teléfono pero no tengo mucho dinero – I would buy a new phone, but I don't have much money

Sería algo un poco más comprensible – It would be something a little bit more understandable

¿Qué Usted aconsejaría a los jóvenes? – What would you advice to young people?

¿Quierías manejar un camion? – Would you like to drive a truck?

Degrees of comparison

In English, one can say "beautiful, more beautiful, the most beautiful" – these are degrees of comparison of the word "beautiful". In Spanish we can say so too.

Let's start from irregulars.

First of all, memorize these two words: BUENO – good, and MAL – bad, because these two words have own irregular degrees of comparison in all (or almost all) languages, including Spanish:

| Bueno – good | Mejor – better | El/la mejor – the best |
| Malo – bad | Peor – worse | El/la peor – the worst |

Also, these are a little bit more irregulars:

Pequeño - little	Menor - less	El/la menor - the least
Joven - young	Menor - younger	El/la menor - the youngest
Viejo - old	Mayor - older	El/la mayor - the oldest

And all other adjectives are declined with the word MÁS – more.

Bonito (m)	Más bonito	El más bonito
Bonita (f)	Más bonita	La más bonita
beautiful	more beautiful	the most beautiful
Grande	Más grande	El/la más grande
big	bigger	the biggest
Fuerte	Más fuerte	El/la más fuerte
strong	stronger	the strongest

Examples

Su Hermana es mayor que la mía – his sister is older than mine

Esta cámara es más costosa que esa – this camera is more expensive than that one

El edificio más alto está en los Emiratos Árabes Unidos – the highest building is (located) in the United Arab Emirates

El inglés es más facíl que el español – English is easier than Spanish

Yo pensaba que ellos eran las personas más estúpidas del mundo, pero me equivoqaba – I thought that they were the most stupid people in the world, but I was mistaken

¿Quén más quiere obtener la oferta más beneficio? – Who else wants to get the most benefit offer?

El ritmo de esa canción es más rápido que de la canción anterior – The rhythm of this song is faster than of the previous one

Los niños tienen menos responsabilidades – Children have less responsibilities

¿Qué cocina es la más favorita por tú mujer? – What cousine is the most favorite for your wife?

Lo peor es que no haciamos nada por tiempo largo – The worst is that we didn't do anything for long time

Quando era el estudiante, lo fue el tiempo más feliz de mi vida – When I was a student, it was it most happy time of my life

Exercises

Conjugate verbs in conditional mood

1. ¿Qué _____ tú en esta situación? (HACER – to do) – What would you do in this situation?
2. ¿Me _____ en este traje? (RECONOCER – to recognize) – Would you recognize me in this suit?
3. ¿Cuánto _____ usted por este apartamento? (PAGAR – to pay) – How much would You pay for this apartment?
4. ¿Cuánto _____ ella en esa tienda? (GASTAR – to spend) – How much would she spend in that store?
5. Ellos _____ nuestras decisiónes (ACCEPTAR – to accept) – They would accept our decisions
6. ¿Qué _____ a tus padres para en la Navidad? (REGALAR – to give a present) – What would you give to your parents in Christmas?
7. A quién _____ ir conmigo a la fiesta? (GUSTAR – to like) – Who would like to go with me to the party?

Use appropriate degree of comparison

8. Mi hija es _____ que su hijo (ALTO – tall) – My daughter is taller than his son
9. ¿Cuál es _____ de los dos? (BUENO – good) – Which one is better of the two?
10. ¿Cuáles naranjas son _____ ? (SABROSO – tasty) – Which oranges are the most tasty?
11. ¿Quién de ustedes es _____? (JOVEN – young) – Which (who) of you is the youngest?
12. Sobre los trenes, es _____ viajar por trenes separados que por los directos (BARATO – cheap) – What about the trains, it is cheaper to travel by separate trains than direct ones.
13. Sus hermanos son _____ que ella (VIEJO – old) – Her brothers are older than she

Answers

1: harías, **2**: reconocerías, **3**: pagaría, **4**: gastaría, **5**: aceptarían, **6**: regalarías, **7**: le gustría, **8**: más alta, **9**: mejor, **10**: las más sabrosas, **11**: el menor, **12**: más barato, **13**: mayor

Lesson 14: Imperative mood

In English, one can say "Do it!" or "Don't do it!" In Spanish, one can say so too. The imperative mood is used to give commands, orders, instructions etc. The imperative mood exists for these pronouns only: Tú, Usted, Nosotoros, Vosotros, and Ustedes. And it has different affirmative and negative forms.

Let's conjugate an –AR verb in the Imperative mood.

Esperar – to wait for, to hope;

	Affirmative	Negative
(Tú)	espera	no esperes
(Usted)	espere	no espere
(Nosotros)	esperemos	no esperemos
(Vosotros)	esperad	no esperéis
(Ustedes)	esperen	no esperen

And one –ER verb. –IR and –ER verbs are conjugated the same in the imperative mood.

Comprender – to understand

	Affirmative	Negative
(Tú)	comprende	no comprendas
(Usted)	comprendas	no comprenda
(Nosotros)	comprendamos	no comprendamos
(Vosotros)	comprended	no comprendáis
(Ustedes)	comprendan	no comprendan

Imperative mood can be used:

For reflexive verbs, one must add an appropriate reflexive pronoun.

Levantarse – to get up:

	Affirmative	Negative
(Tú)	levanta<u>te</u>	no <u>te</u> levantes
(Usted)	levanta<u>te</u>	no <u>se</u> levante
(Nosotros)	levanté<u>monos</u>	no <u>nos</u> levantemos
(Vosotros)	levanta<u>os</u>	no <u>os</u> levantéis
(Ustedes)	levánten<u>se</u>	no <u>se</u> levanten

Also, the indirect or direct pronouns are added after ending in the affirmative form, but not in the negative:

Comprende<u>lo</u> – find it (command Tú)

No <u>lo</u> comprendas – don't understand it

Esperad<u>me</u> por favor – wait me please (command Vosotros)

No <u>me</u> esperad por favor – don't wait me please

¡Despiertame temprano por la mañana! – Wake me up early in the morning!

¡No me despiertes temprano! – Don't wake me up early!

Also, there are irregular verbs too. First of all, we have to consider SER and IR, because they are the most irregular two:

Ser – to be

	Affirmative	Negative
(Tú)	sé	no seas
(Usted)	sea	no sea
(Nosotros)	seamos	no seamos
(Vosotros)	sed	no seáis
(Ustedes)	sean	sean

Ir – to go

	Affirmative	Negative
(Tú)	ve	no vayas
(Usted)	vaya	no vaya
(Nosotros)	vamos*, vayamos	no vayamos
(Vosotros)	<u>id</u>	no vayáis
(Ustedes)	vayan	no vayan

*-VAMOS is equivalent of English "Let's" or "Let's go".

Rules for other irregular verbs:

The affirmative form of VOSOTROS is always regular for all verbs.

Irregular affirmative commands TÚ of these verbs should just be memorized:

Decir – (Tú) di

Salir – (Tú) sal

Hacer –(Tú) haz

Poner – (Tú) pon

Tener – (Tú) ten

Venir – (Tú) ven

For verbs that have a change in stem in present tense, for example: Encontrar – to find, Yo enc<u>ue</u>ntro – I find, stem ENC<u>UE</u>NTR-, the imperative form will have this change too, apart from Nosotros and Vosotros commands:

	Affirmative	Negative
(Tú)	enc<u>ue</u>ntra	no enc<u>ue</u>ntres
(Usted)	enc<u>ue</u>ntre	no enc<u>ue</u>ntre
(Nosotros)	encontremos	no encontremos
(Vosotros)	encontrad	no encontréis
(Ustedes)	enc<u>ue</u>ntren	no enc<u>ue</u>ntren

And for the verbs that end in –GO or –ZCO at conjugation with YO in present tense, for example:

Salir – to leave, Yo sal<u>go</u> – I leave, stem SALG-
Parecer – to look, Yo pare<u>zco</u> – I look, stem PAREZC-

the affirmative commands USTED, NOSOTROS, USTEDES, and all negative commands will have this stem.

	Affirmative	Negative
(Tú)	conoce	conozcas
(Usted)	conozca	conozca
(Nosotros)	conozcamos	conozcamos
(Vosotros)	conoced	conozcáis
(Ustedes)	conozcan	conozcan

Conjugate these regular verbs in imperative mood and build sentences with them:

Quedar – to stay/to remain
Llevar – to carry/to bring
Mirar – to watch/to look at
Recibir – to receive
Existir – to exist
Considerar – to consider

Entrar – to enter
Presentar – to present
Crear – to create
Levantarse – to get up
Permitir – to permit
Irse – to leave

And these irregular ones:

With stem change
Dormir – to sleep,
Jugar – to play,
Entender – to understand,
Pensar – to think,
Cerrar – to close

With –go/zco
Parecer – to look like,
Aparecer – appear,
Oír – to hear,
Desaparecer – to disappear.

Examples:

¡No te vayas! – don't leave!

¡Escúchame! – Listen me!

Llevenlo (ustedes) aquí por favor, tengo que comprobarlo – Bring it here please, I have to check it

Haz esta tarea en mí lugar – do this task instead of me

¡No parece una idiota! – don't look like an idiot!

¡Vota por ese candidato en las elecciones! – vote for this candidate in the elections!

¡Vamos a bailar! – let's dance!

¡Vayamos a la fiesta! – let's go to the party?

Para comprenderlo, lee este libro – In order to understand it, read that book

¡Haz algo para mí! – do something for me!

Hablad con ellos, quizás dirán que necectáis – speak with them, maybe they will say what you need

¡Calmate y disfruta! – Calm yourself and enjoy!

Build sentences with these words:

El sofá – sofa	el tiempo – time	la mujer – woman/wife
la silla – chair	el banco – bank	la moneda – coin/currency
la bañera – bath	la hija – daughter	la cuenta – account
el padre – father	el hijo – son	la tarjeta de crédito – credit card
hombre – man	el primo - cousin	

Adverbs

English adverbs are formed by adding –ly, and Spanish adverbs are formed by adding –**MENTE** to its **FEMINIE** FORM:

Claro(m), Clar<u>a</u>(f) – clear, Clara<u>mente</u> – clearly

Extraño(m), Extrañ<u>a</u>(f) – strange, Extraña<u>mente</u> – strangely

Posible(m/f) – possible, Posible<u>mente</u> - possibly

Frequente(m/f) – frequent, Frecuente<u>mente</u> – frequently

Exceptional adverbs that have own form:

Despacio – slowly, Bastante – quite, Demasiado – too much, Mal – badly, Poco – little, Mucho – a lot, Temprano – early, Cada vez más – increasingly.

Examples:

La música está bastante rudiosa – The music is too loud

Ella rápidamente contestó – She quickly answered

Diego exitosamente vendió su auto – Diego successfully sold his car

Actualmente lo se hace muy fácil – Actually one does it very easy

Cuándo Sofia acabó de trabajar, inmediatamente corrió a la reunión con su amiga – When Sofia finished working, she immediately ran to meeting with her friend

No lo consideres frívolamente – Don't consider it frivolously

¡No pasen de largo indiferentemente! – Don't pass by indifferently!

Te extraño mucho – I miss you a lot *(extrañar is verb meaning "to miss")*

When a verbs is modified by two or more adverbs at the same time, only the last one will have the ending –MENTE and all previous will be in FEMININE form:

Gabriel se accostumbró a nueva ocupación tranquila y fácilmente – Gabriel got used to new occupation calmly and easily

La playa estaba llena de gente muy rápida y locamente cada día en el verano – The beach got filled by people very fast and crazily everyday in the summer

El doctor cuidada y precisamente verificó el paciente – The doctor carefully and accurately checked the patient

¡Léelo rudiosa y atencionalmente por favor! – Read it loudly and attencionally please!

Exercises
Conjugate verbs in imperative mood

1. ¡_____ a las ocho! (LEVANTARSE – to get up, command TÚ) – Get up at eight o'clock!
2. ¡No _____ la puerta por favor! (CERRAR – to close, command USTED) – Don't close the door please!
3. ¡No _____ hoy! (IRSE – to leave, command USTEDES) – Don't leave today!
4. ¡_____ con nosotros! (JUGAR – to play, command VOSOTROS) – Play with us!
5. ¡_____ a la fiesta! (IR – to go, command NOSOTROS) – Let's go to the party!
6. ¡No_____ nada! (DECIR – to say, command TÚ) – Don't say anything!
7. ¿_____ algunos amigos? (LLAMAR – to call, command NOSOTROS) – Let's call some friends?
8. Tengo una solicitud para ti, _____ hoy por favor (AYUDAR – to help, command TÚ) – I have a request for you, <u>help her</u> please today
9. ¡Niños,_____ a la casa por el almuerzo! (CORRER – to run, command VOSOTROS) – Kids, run home for lunch!
10. ¡_____ el teléfono! (CARGAR – to charge, command USTED) – Charge the phone!
11. ¡_____ esto! (DAR – to give, command TÚ) – <u>Give me</u> this!
12. ¡No _____ ese movimiento! (SIGUIR – to follow, command VOSOTROS) – Don't follow this movement!
13. ¡_____ por ella (HACER – to do, command TÚ) – Do it for her!
14. ¡No _____ tarde! (LEVANTARSE – to get up) – Don't get up late!
15. _____ su estatura Usted por favor (MEDIR* – to measure, *- stem MÍD-) – Measure your stature please

Answers

1: levánta<u>te</u>, **2**: cierre, **3**: se vayan, **4**: jugad, **5**: vamos, **6**: digas, **7**: llamamos, **8**: ayúda<u>le</u>, **9**: corred, **10**: carga, **11**: da<u>me</u>, **12**: siguéis, **13**: haz<u>lo</u>, **14**: te levantes, **15**: míde

Lesson 15. Progressive tense and present tense participles

The progressive tense in Spanish is almost the same as in English. In English, we can say "I do" and "I am doing", where "I am doing" is the progressive form. In Spanish, the progressive tenses are formed by combining the verb ESTAR – to be and a present tense participle:

ESTAR + present PARTICIPLE

Present tense participle:

Spanish present tense participle is equivalent of English –ING form of verb.

For –AR verbs, change the ending to –ANDO

For –ER and –IR verbs, change the ending to –IENDO

Hablar – to speak, Hablando – speaking

Hacer – to do, Haciendo – doing

Servir – to serve, Sirviendo – serving

Romparse – to get broken, rompandose – being broken (reflexive)

Generally, all you need to know for the progressive tense is conjugation of ESTAR in all previously considered tenses (present, past I, past II, future, conditional mood).

Here are the examples with the pronoun Yo – I for all previously considered tenses:

Yo estoy escribiendo – I am writing

Yo estaba jugando – I was playing

Yo estuve aprendiendo – I was learning

Yo estaré cocinando – I will be cooking

Yo estaría manejando – I would be driving

Form present tense participles out of these verbs and conjugate them in all tenses with all pronouns and build sentences:

mover – to move	vaciar – to empty	cambiar – to change
mirar – to look at	acabar – to finish	involucrar – to involve
mirarse – to look	ofrecer – to offer	gastar – to spend (money)
nadar – to swim	combatir – to fight	mudarse – to move oneself
oler – to smell	luchar – to struggle	pasar – to spend (time)/to pass
reír – to laugh	ofender – to offend	

Irregulars:

Irregular participles have **the same letter in stem as in the Past tense II.** E.g. Rep<u>i</u>tió – he repeated, Rep<u>i</u>tiendo – repeating.

Dormir – to sleep, D<u>u</u>rmiendo - sleeping

Mentir – to lie, M<u>i</u>ntiendo – lying

Decir – to say, D<u>i</u>ciendo – saying

Venir – to come, V<u>i</u>niendo – coming

Ir – to go, <u>Y</u>endo – going (exception). *Ser* and *estar* have regular form.

Examples:

Yo estuve reparando mi bicicleta durante tres horas – I was repairing my bicycle during three hours

Nuestros amigos estarán mudándose el proximo mes – Our friends will move (themselves) next month

Mi cerveza está acabándose – My beer is getting finished

Trabajando aquí, yo me canso – Working here, I get tired

Usted encontrará la entrada a la izquierda del lugar dónde está estando de pie ahora mismo – You will find the entrance in the left of the place where you are standing right now

El fotógrafo estuvo tomando las fotos de un model en una sesión de fotos – The photographer was taking hotos of a model in a photo session

Buscando los anteojos, Maria encontré muchas otras cosas – Looking for the glasses, Maria has found many other things

Other forms progressive tenses

Progressive tenses can be formed not only with ESTAR, but also with the following verbs:

- **LLEVAR + PARTICIPLE** – to have been doing something. Analogue of English perfect progressive tenses (which are with "have been"). Literally this verb means "To carry"

David lleva cuatro años aprendiendo Chino – David has been learning Chinese for four years

Esta estación de metro lleva funcionando desde dos mil quince – This metro station has been functioning since 2015

Llevo dos horas esperando a mi amigo al lado del bar – I have been waiting my friend for two hours next to the bar

- **VENIR + PARTICIPLE** – to have been doing something (as well as Llevar + participle)

La capacidad de la sala se vino disminuyendo a medida que lo estuvo llenandose por la gente – Capacity of the hall has been decreasing as it was filling by people

Vengo jugando los juegos en línea desde la infancia – I have been playing online games since childhood

Viene trabajando por la campañía de envios desde mil novecientos noventa y ocho – He has been working for the shipping company since 1998

- **IR + PARTICIPLE** – to be (gradually) doing something.

Mi hermano va limpiando la habitación – My brother is cleaneaning the room (gradually)

El viajero se va preparando para salir mañana – The traveler is preparing to leave tomorrow

Para suceder en algo, hay que ir haciendo los pasos pequeños cada día sin dejar – In order to succeed in something, one must be doing small steps everyday without giving up

- **SEGUIR + PARTICIPLE** – to be doing something (continuously). Basically, the verb SEGUIR means "to follow/to continue/to go on/to continue doing sth." This construction is used to describe a continuing action.

El tiempo sigue pasando – Time is passing by

Sigue nevando – It's snowing

La clima siguió cambiandose – The weather was changing

- **ANDAR + PARTICIPLE** – to be doing something. This construction is used to describe an action in process. Basically ANDAR means "to walk".

-¿Qué él está haciendo? -Anda leyendo una instrucción – What is he doing? He is reading an instruction

Alguien creyó que la época de las computadores se andó acabando pero se equivoqaba – Someone believed that the age of computers was finishing but they were mistaken

Andamos participando en la conferencia durante toda la semana – We were participating in the conference during the whole week

Build sentences with these words:

el oso – bear	el puente – bridge	el objetivo – aim/goal
lento – slow	la ropa – clothes	la avenida – avenue
el ruido – noise	la puerta – door	simultáneo – simultaneous
limpio – clean	el sonido – sound	la estación – station
el barco – ship	la calle – street	anterior – previous
entero – entire	el boleto – ticket	la almohada – pillow
el mar – sea	el cerebro – brain	confiable – trustworthy
sucio – dirty	el cuerpo – body	la victoria – victory
azul – blue	jardín – garden	el río - river

Exercises

Use verbs in progressive tense conjugating ESTAR with participle out of given verbs.

1. ¿Cuándo _____? (ACABAR – to finish) – When will you(tú) be finishing?
2. ¿Qué _____? (HACER – to do) – What are you doing?
3. Yo_____ la casa (CONSTRUIR – to build) – I am building the house
4. _____ la habitación cuando estabas ocupado (LIMPIAR – to clean) – We were cleaning the room when you were busy
5. Juan _____ a las diez (DORMIR – to sleep) – Juan was sleeping at 10 o'clock
6. Unas chicas _____ al cielo en la tarde (MIRAR – to look) – Some girls were looking at the sky at evening
7. _____ hasta que me llamaste (COSER – to sew) – I was sewing until you called me
8. Nosotros _____ a la casa nueva la semana pasada (MUDARSE – to move) – We were moving to new home in the previous week
9. Cuando estábamos en París, _____ muchas fotos (TOMAR – to take) – When we were in Paris, we were taking a lot of photos
10. El candidato _____ las elecciónes (GANAR – to win) – The candidate was winning the elections
11. ¿Dónde ustedes _____ hace una hora? (ESTAR – to be) – Where have you been one hour ago?
12. _____ y _____ en la fiesta, él se emborrachó (BAILAR – do dance, BEBER – to drink) – Dancing and drinking in the party he got drunk

Answers

1: estarás acabando, **2**: estás haciendo, **3**: estoy construyendo, **4**: estábamos limpiando, **5**: estaba durmiendo, **6**: estuvieron mirando, **7**: estaba cosiendo, **8**: estuvimos mudándonos, **9**: estuvimos tomando, **10**: estuvo ganando, **11**: estuvieron estando, **12**: bailando, bebiendo

Lesson 16: Past participles, HABER and perfective tenses

In English one can say "do – done, write – written", where "done" and "written" are **past tense participles.** In Spanish regular past tense participles are formed by changing a verb's ending to:

-ADO for –AR verbs,

-IDO for –ER and –IR verbs.

Pasar – to pass, Pasado – passed

Comer – to eat, Comido – eaten

Incluir – to include, Incluido – included

And there are some exceptions:

Escribir – to write, Escrito – written

Hacer – to do, Echo – done

Poner – to put, Puesto – put

Morir – to die, Muerto – dead

Decir – say, Dicho – said

Satisfacer – to satisfy, Satisfecho – satisfied

Ver – to see, Visto – seen

Volver – to return, Vuelto – returned

Abrir – to open, Abierto – opened

Romper – to break, Roto – broken

Resolver – to resolve, Resuelto – resolved

Cubrir – to cover, Cubierto – covered

Completar – to complete, Completo - completed

And the participles can have gender and plural endings:

Cerrar – to close, participles: Cerrado (m), cerrada (f), cerrados (m, pl), cerradas (f, pl)

91

Examples

La novela fue escrita por el escritor famoso – The novel was written by the famous writer

La comida seré cocinada pronto – The food will be cooked soon

¿Qué fue construido en tú ciudad recientemente? – What was built in your city recently?

Perfective tenses

The perfective tenses consist of the verb HABER conjugated in an appropriate tense and a past tense participle, or if to say it simpler:

HABER + PAST TENSE PARTICIPLE

The perfective Spanish tenses are equivalent of English perfective tenses like "I have done, I had done, I will have done, I would have done". Notice, that the word "have" is not "tener" here despite it means "to have".

Some keywords for perfective tenses	
Esta semana – this week	Ya – already
Este año – this year	Todavía – still
Este mes – this month	Aún – yet
Hoy – today	En cuanto – as soon as

The verb HABER

HABER is a special verb that has two general ways of use:

- As an auxiliary verb to form a perfect tense, like English tense "I have done", where "have" is equivalent of Spanish HABER.

- A verb for expressing existence of something, like "there is/are, there were, there will be".

First of all, look at the table of its conjugation in all previously considered tenses:

	Present	**Past I**	**Past II**
Yo	he	había	hube
Tú	has	habías	hubiste

Él, ella, usted	ha, hay*	había	hubo
Nosotros	hemos	habíamos	hubimos
Vosotros	habéis	habíais	hubisteis
Ellos, ustedes	han	habían	hubieron

*HAY – this form is used to say "there is/are", check the next section.

	Future	**Conditional**
Yo	habré	habría
Tú	habrás	habrías
Él, ella, usted	habré	habría
Nosotros	habremos	habríamos
Vosotros	habréis	habríais
Ellos, ustedes	habrán	habrán

Examples

Present perfect tense:

Yo lo he acabado ya – I have finished it already

Nosotros no hemos visitado Estados Unidos todavía – We have not visited USA still

El gato ha comido tres veces hoy – The cat has eaten three time today

Nuestros padres no han ido al mar este año – Our parents have not gone to the sea this year

Unos estudiantes han conversado con el profesor hoy – Some students have talked to the profesor today

El vendedor ha recibido su salario – The seller has received his salary

¿Qué vosotros esta semana? – What have you done this week?

Past perfect tense:

Cuando vine a la casa, mi mujer había cocinado la cena para mí – When I've come come, my wife had cooked a dinner for me

¿Le decimos a quién lo había escrito antes que nosotros? – Who had written it before we said it?

Durante dos meses este hombre había trabajado en la fábrica – During two months this man had been working in the factory

Ella y su marido habían estudiado en la universidad hasta el fin del año – She and he husband had been studying in the university until the end of the year

Después de que Luís había leído tu pregunta, se fue a consultarla en internet – After that Luis had read your question, he went to consult her in internet

Past perfect II (preterite perfect):

Después de que hubimos completado la tarea, ella llamó al jefe – After we had completed the task, she called the boss

Cuando mis amigos hubieron llegado, fuimos a jugar al fútbol – When my friends had arrived, we went to play football

Tan pronto nos hubiste dejado, empezamos trabajar – As soon as you left us, we started to work

Hube resuelto la tarea antes de que lección comenzara – I had solved this task before the lecture began

Yo hube de leerla un par de veces para entenderla – I had to read it a couple of times to understand it

Future perfect

¿Tú habrás venido a las nueve? – Will you have come until 9 o'clock?

Habremos tratado repararlo hoy – We will have tried to repair it today

Habré aprendido el idioma ruso antes del fin del año – I will have learned the Russian language before the end of the year

¿Ustedes se habrán mudado a Alemania en un año? – Will You move to Germany in one year?

Conditional

Yo habría vivido en este país por unos años – I would have lived in this country for a some years

Habríamos comprado un auto costoso si habría tenido un unos buenos negocios – We would have bought an expensive car if we had a good business

Mi amiga habría aprendido tocar la guitarra si hubiese tenido tiempo – My friend would have learned to play guitar if she had time

There is/are/were/will be

In Spanish language "There is/are/were/will be" are formed by forms of the verb HABER.

Hay – there is/are

Había, hubo – there was

Había, hubieron – there were

Habré – there will be

Habrá – there will be (plural)

Habría – there would be

Examples

Hay dos platos en la mesa – There are two plates on the table

¿Qué había construido en aquel lugar hace dos años? – What was built two years ago?

Habrá cinco estaciones nuevas de metro en nuestra ciudad en tres años – There will be five new metro stations in our city in three years

Hay más de ciento de ciudades en este país – There are more than one hundred cities in this country

Como recuerdo, siempre había los boletos baratos a este destino – As I remember, there have always been cheap tickets to this destination

Hubo un restaurante bueno en esta calle – There was a good restaurant on this street

Build sentences with these words:

la torre – tower	La ventana – window	azul – blue	el cielo – sky
la lluvia – rain	El sitio web – website	el sol – sun	la nube – cloud
la luna – moon	amarillo – yellow	gris – gray	

Exercises

Use appropriate form of perfective tense.

1. ¿Por qué no lo _____ por un tiempo largo? (COMPRENDER – to understand) – Why have we not been understanding it for long time?
2. Yo lo _____ desde dos mil cinco! (DECIR – to say) – I have been saying that since 2012!
3. ¿Por qué _____ aquí? (ESPERAR – to wait for) – Why have you(tú) waited for us here?
4. El compositor famoso _____ muchas canciones (CREAR – to create) – The famous composer has created many songs
5. La fábrica _____ dos mil computadoras (PRODUCIR – to produce) – The factory has produced two thousand computers
6. La impresora _____ tres cientos papeles ayer (IMPRIMIR – to print) – The printer has printed three hundred papers yesterday
7. La locomotora _____ a la mitad del camino (ROMPERSE – to get broken) – The locomotive has got broken in the half of the way
8. Si hubiese sido* candidato la presidencia _____ muchos cambios? (PROMETER – to promise) – If you(tú) were a presidential candidate, would you have promised many changes?
   *- this is SER in subjunctive mood, learn more in the next lesson
9. Este mes nuestra empresa _____ el lucro (DOBLAR – to double) – This month our company has doubled the profit
10. _____ esta tarea hoy? (COMPLETAR – to complete) – Would you have completed this task today?
11. Son las siete de la mañana y no _____ nada (DORMIR – to sleep) – It is 7 o'clock of morning and I have not slept at all

Answers

1: hemos comprendido, **2**: he dicho, **3**: nos has esperado, **4**: ha creado, **5**: ha producido, **6**: hubo imprimido, **7**: se ha roto, **8**: habrías prometido, **9**: ha doblado, **10**: habrías completo, **11**: he dormido

Lesson 17: Subjunctive mood

All tenses what we considered before are tenses in indicative mood. And now we will consider the tenses in Subjunctive mood. Yes, the Spanish language is rich in tenses.

There is subjective mood in English too, we use it when we say: "If I were...", "I wish that he do...". However in English it is not used as widely as in Spanish. The Subjunctive mood is not a tense but mood, but grammatically, it looks like the whole bunch of tenses, so it requires time investment to learn and practice.

So let's figure out, what is the sense of subjunctive mood. **Subjunctive mood describes an action that doesn't actually happen or take place, or hypothetical situation, or doubt, or wish, or emotion, i.e – not certain actions.** In order to make it more clear for understanding, look at the comparative examples, the conjugation of verbs will be considered later:

Él hace – he does; this is indicative mood, because the action "he does" actually happens, this is certain fact.

Dudo que él haga – I doubt that he do; this is subjunctive mood, because the action "he does" doesn't actually happen, but I doubt about it – uncertain fact.

Cuando él era joven, le gustaba nadar – When he was young, he loved to swim; this is indicative mood, because it describes an exact fact that took place in the past ("when he was young" - certain fact)

Si él fuese joven, le gustaría nadar – If he were young, he would love to swim; This is subjunctive mood, because it describes not a certain fact but what didn't actually took place in the past, "if he were" instead of "if he was".

Era major porque ella nos escuchaba – It was better because she listened to us; This is indicative mood, because the action (she listened to us) actually happened.

Esto sería mejor si ella nos escuchara – It would be better if she listened to us; This is subjunctive mood, because the action (IF she listened to us) didn't, actually happen, but "it would be better if it happened"

Of you understood the logic of subjunctive mood, let's learn more about conjugation. The conjugation of verbs in subjunctive mood is quite similar to usual indicative mood.

Cantar – to sing, this is –AR verb.

Present tense

	Indicative	Subjunctive
Yo	canto	cante
Tú	cantas	cantes
Él, ella, usted	canta	cante
Nosotros	cantamos	cantemos
Vosotros	cantáis	cantéis
Ellos, ustedes	cantan	canten

Past tense I (Pretérito imperfect)

	Indicative	Subjunctive
Yo	cantaba	cantara
Tú	cantabas	cantaras
Él, ella, usted	cantaba	cantara
Nosotros	cantábamos	cantáramos
Vosotros	cantabais	cantarais
Ellos, ustedes	cantaban	cantaran

Past tense II (Pretérito perfecto simple)

	Indicative	Subjunctive
Yo	canté	cantase
Tú	cantaste	cantases
Él, ella, usted	cantó	cantase
Nosotros	cantamos	cantásemos
Vosotros	cantasteis	cantaseis
Ellos, ustedes	cantaron	cantasen

And in future tense the subjunctive mood is not used. It is used only in legal documentation, so we will not consider it.

And let's consider one more verb. –ER and –IR verbs are conjugated the same as subjunctive.

Describir – to describe, this is –IR verb.

Present tense

	Indicative	Subjunctive
Yo	describo	describa
Tú	describes	describas
Él, ella, usted	describe	describa
Nosotros	describimos	describamos
Vosotros	describís	describáis
Ellos, ustedes	describen	describan

Past tense I (Pretérito imperfect)

	Indicative	Subjunctive
Yo	describía	describiera
Tú	describías	describieras
Él, ella, usted	describía	describiera
Nosotros	describíamos	describiéramos
Vosotros	describíais	describierais
Ellos, ustedes	describían	describieran

Past tense II (Pretérito perfecto simple)

	Indicative	Subjunctive
Yo	describí	describiese
Tú	describiste	describieses
Él, ella, usted	describió	describiese
Nosotros	describimos	describiésemos
Vosotros	describisteis	describieseis
Ellos, ustedes	describieron	describiesen

There are irregular verbs here too. First of all let's conjugate the most irregular verbs SER and IR , they require memorization:

Present tense

	Ser	**Ir**
Yo	sea	vaya
Tú	seas	vayas
Él, ella, usted	sea	vaya
Nosotros	seamos	vayamos
Vosotros	seáis	vayáis
Ellos, ustedes	sean	vayan

Past tense I (Pretérito imperfect)

	Ser	**Ir**
Yo	fuera	fuera
Tú	fueras	fueras
Él, ella, usted	fueras	fueras
Nosotros	fuéramos	fuéramos
Vosotros	fuerais	fuerais
Ellos, ustedes	fueran	fueran

Past tense II (Pretérito perfecto simple)

	Ser	**Ir**
Yo	fuese	fuese
Tú	fueses	fueses
Él, ella, usted	fuese	fuese
Nosotros	fuésemos	fuésemos
Vosotros	fueseis	fueseis
Ellos, ustedes	fuesen	fuesen

As you can see, the conjugation of SER and IR matches in both past tenses.

Other irregular verbs have common characteristics:

Conjugate an irregular verb in usual present tense with the pronoun YO. For example HACER – to do: YO HAGO – I do. And the stem in present tense subjunctive will be the same as the stem in usual present tense with pronoun YO, i.e. HAG-. In this case the conjugation in subjunctive will be: YO HAGA, TÚ HAGAS, ÉL HAGA etc. It's the same for all other irregular verbs.

Conocer – to know, subjunctive stem CONOZC –

Poder – can, subjunctive stem PUED-

Tener – to have, subjunctive stem TENG-

Decir – to say, subjunctive stem DIG-

Oír – to hear, subjunctive stem OIG-

Ver – to se, subjunctive stem VE-

Saber – to know, subjunctive stem SEP-

And so on for all irregular verbs.

In past tense, the situation is quite similar. All irregular verbs in subjunctive forms in both past tenses will have the same stem as in indicative **Past tense II.** For example, ESTAR – to be, stem in past II is ESTUV-, so the stem in past subjunctive will be also ESTUV-: YO ESTUVIERA, TÚ ESTUVIERAS etc. or YO ESTUVIESE, TÚ ESTUVIESES etc.

Querer – to want, past subjunctive stem QUIS-

Poder – can, past subjunctive stem PUD-

Saber – to know, past subjunctive stem SUP-

And so on for all irregular verbs.

Conjugate verbs from the previous lessons in subjunctive mood.

Build sentences with these words:

posible – possible	probable – probable	el contador – accountant
famoso – famous	bajo – low	imposible – impossible
solo – single/alone	viejo – old	vacío – empty
limpio – clean	medio – middle	el negocio - business

Examples

Deceamos que tuviéramos un yate – We wish we had a yacht

Quiero que tú me abraces – I want you to hug me

Ojalá este estante no se caiga – Hopefully, this shelf won't fall

¿Por qué ellos quieren que seamos débiles? – Why they want us to be weak?

Si estos estudiantes fuesen inteligentes, resolverían esta tarea más rápido – If these students were smart, they would solve this task faster

Es possible que ella me enviase una carta – It is possible that she sent me a letter

En caso de que lo comprobes, dime – In case you check it, tell me

¡Si fuera joven, tendría más energía! – If I were young, I would have more energy

Te pido que me ayudes con eso – I ask you to help me with that

Es probable que el mensajero no venga – The courier probably don't come

Es necesario que vosotros leéis los términos de uso – It is necessary that you read the terms of use

Tal vez lo tuviera una ventaja – Maybe it had an advantage

Te deseo que tengas feliz Año Nuevo – I wish you to have happy New Year

Quizás te sentirás mejor si tomes unas pastillas – Maybe you will feel better if you take some pills

Creo que ella parezca linda – I believe that she looks cute

No te recomiendo que nades en este río – I don't recommend you to swim in this river

No me llamas antes de que lo completes – Don't call me until you complete it

Ellos permiten que sus hijos vengan aquí – They allow their children to come

Exercises
Conjugate verbs in subjunctive mood
1. Quiero que _____ inteligente (SER – to be) – I want you(tú) to be smart
2. Pienso que _____ hacerlo (PODER – can) – I think that we could do it
3. Ojalá mi hermano no _____ a fumar (EMPEZAR – to start) – Hopefully my brother doesn't start to smoke
4. No creo que él _____ romper la pared (PODER – can) – I don't believe that he can break the wall
5. Me gustaría que este candidato _____ (ELEGIRSE – to get elected) – I wish that this candidate get elected
6. Supongo que el futbolista _____ marcar el gol (PODER – can) – I suppose that the football player could hit the goal
7. Espero que mis hijos _____ un educación bueno (OBTENER – to obtain) – I hope that my children get a good education

Figure out whether you need to use the subjunctive mood or no, and use appropriate conjugation
8. Ojalá ellos no los _____ (ATACAR – to attack) – Hopefully they don't attack them
9. Tal vez _____ aquí muchos veces (APARECER – to appear) – Maybe it appeared here many times
10. Quiero _____ piloto de un avión (SER – to be) – I want to be a pilot of an airplane
11. Ella espera que su marido _____ un trabajo (ENCONTRAR – to find) – She hopes that her husband finds a job
12. Parece que él _____ de sí mismo (OLVIDARSE – to forget oneself) – It seems that he forgot himself
13. Yo ví cómo la policía _____ a un ladrón (DETENER – to detain) – I saw how the police detained a robber
14. ¿Cuándo _____ a la universidad? (VOLVER – to get back) – When you get back to the university?

Answers
1: seas, **2**: pudimos, **3**: empiece, **4**: pueda, **5**: fuese elegido, **6**: pudiese, **7**: obtengan, **8**: ataquen, **9**: apareció, **10**: ser, **11**: encuentre, **12**: se olvidó **13**: detuvo, **14**: volverás

Lesson 18. Perfect subjunctive

In the previous lessons we learned about perfect tenses subjunctive mood. The perfect subjunctive is used in the same types and clauses as non-perfect subjunctive.

The formula of perfect subjunctive is also the same:

HABER + past PARTICIPLE

In order to form perfective form of subjunctive, all you need to know is conjugation of HABER in subjunctive mood:

Present tense

Yo	haya
Tú	hayas
Él, ella, usted	haya
Nosotros	hayamos
Vosotros	hayáis
Ellos, ustedes	hayan

	Past I	Past II
Yo	hubiera	hubiese
Tú	hubieras	hubieses
Él, ella, usted	hubiera	hubiese
Nosotros	hubiéramos	hubiésemos
Vosotros	hubierais	hubieseis
Ellos, ustedes	hubieran	hubiesen

Examples

Ellos esperan que tú hayas salido temprano – They hope that you have left early

Si mi hermana lo hubiera sabido, yo le habría preguntado – If my sister had known it, I would have asked her

Se podría haber sido mejor si hubieses movido la mesa ahí – It would be better if you have moved the table there

Mi madre dudó que yo hubiese ido a la escuela – My mom doubted that I went to school

Es posible que ella me hubiera llamado – It is possible that she has called me

No estoy seguro que ellos hubieran vivido en Estados Unidos – I am not sure that they have lived in United States

No es verdad que Juan haya estado en esa conferencia – It is not true that Juan has been to this conference

Su profesor recomienda que lo hayamos leído – Their professor recommends that we have read it

¿Si hubieses tenido el dinero ayer podrías haber ido con nosotros? – If you had money yesterday, would you be able to go with us?

Si hubieses estudiado más español, ahora entenderías mejor – If you had studied more Spanish, now you would understand better

El jefe duda que haya tomado un buen decisión – The boss doubts that he has taken a good decision

Es bueno que hayas ganado el concurso – It is good that you have won the contest

Build sentences with there words:

el rey – king
la reina – queen
el reino – kingdom
el estado – state
unido – united
la unión – union

el papel – paper
el documento – document
simple – simple
temprano – early
gratis – free
suficiente – enough

105

Exercises

Use appropriate form of perfective subjunctive mood

1. ¿Si _____ aquí, qué harías? (ESTAR – to be) – If you(tú) were here, what would you do?
2. Quiero que lo _____ (SABER – to know) – I want You(Ustedes) to have known it
3. Ojalá ellos lo _____ (TERMINAR – to end) – Hopefully they have ended it
4. Tal vez Daniela _____ el dinero (GASTAR – to spend) – Maybe Daniela has spent the money
5. Quiero creer que mi hijo _____ una vez como hacerlo (OÍR – to hear) – I want to believe that my son has heard once how to do it
6. Es posible él no _____ todavía (DESPERTARSE – to wake up) – It is possible that he has not woken up yet
7. Espero que ellos ya _____ (REUNIRSE – to meet) – I hope that they have already met
8. No estamos seguros si nuestros trabajadores _____ los juegos de computadora en el lugar de haber trabajado hoy (JUGAR – to play) – We are not sure that our employees have played computer games in the workplace today
9. Es posible que ellos nos _____ pero no lo dijeron (RECONOCER – to recognize) – It is possible that they had recognized us but didn't say that
10. Ojalá que tu madre _____ el dinero de tu hermano (ESCONDER – to hide) – Hopefully his mother had hidden the money from your brother
11. Todos dudan que el president _____ la promesa como lo describió (CUMPLIR – to fulfill) – Everybody doubt that the president has fulfilled the promise how he described it

Answers

1: hubieses estado, **2:** hubiesen sabido, **3:** hubieran/hubiesen terminado, **4:** hubiera/hubiese gastado, **5:** hubiera/hubiese oído, **6:** se haya despertado, **7:** se hayan reunido, **8:** hayan jugado, **9:** hubieran/hubiesen reconocido, **10:** hubiera/hubiese escondido, **11:** haya cumplido

Lesson 19: Diminutives

There are diminutive suffixes in English language too, but they are used just in some words. Some of them are:

Kitten – kitt*y*, Jim – Jim*my*, Charles – Charl*ie*

In Spanish language these suffixes can be –ITO(m) and –ITA(f), -CITO(m), -CITA(f), -ITITO(m), -ITITA(f).

Gato – gat*ito* - cat(m)

Gata – gat*ita* - cat(f)

Chico – chiqu*ito* – guy

Chica – chiqu*ita* – chiqu*itita* - girl

Pequeño – pequeñ*ito* – small

Ingrid – Ingridcita – Ingrid(name)

Poco – poqu*ito* – poqu*itito* – little

Also,

There is the postfix –ISIMO for adjectives, this postfix empowers meaning of an adjective:

Bueno – good, buenísimo – so good/the best!

Grande – big, grandísimo – so big/great!

Examples

Su perrita es linda – Her dog is cute

Hay poquitas monedas en la cajita, puedes sacarlas – There are just a few coins in the small box, you can take them

¿Dónde está mi bolsita? – Where is my bag?

¡Tu idea es buenísima! – Your idea is so good!

¿Cómo está tu hijita? – How is your daughter?

Dame un besito – Give me a kiss

¡Comprame um heladito por favor! – Buy me an ice cream please!

Lesson 20: Important verbs and verbal constructions

How to say "To become" or The verbs of change

There are some different ways to say "Become", "to get ...", "to turn into". Notice, that English translation is not always literal:

- **VOLVERSE – to become/to turn into. Sudden changes, Emphasizes contrast between things in the past and in the present.**

Su negocio se volvió exitoso despues de tres meses – His business became successful after three months

Nuestro mundo se vuelve cada vez más complejo – Our world becomes increasingly more complex

El hombre pobre se volvió rico de repente – The poor man suddenly became rich

- **TRANSFORMARSE EN - this verb is used in complete, radical changes, transformations, global changes, physical changes.**

El agua se ha transformado en hielo – Water has turned into ice

¡El niño se transformó en monstruo! – The child became a monster!

Despues de cinco días, estes materiales de construcción se han transformado en la casa nueva – After five days these building materials have been turned into the new house

- **CONVERTIRSE EN - this construction is used for radical changes in profession, occupation, in life.**

El mensajero se convirtió en logístico – The courier became a logistician

Es muy bueno por tus padres que te has convertido en que te quisieron que fueras – It is very good for your parents that you became who they wanted you to be

Juan se convirtió en músico – Juan became a musician

- **PONERSE** – this word is used for temporal changes, for example health changes and changes of state of mind

Marco se puso enojado ayer cuándo yo rompí su computadora – Marco became angry yesterday when I broke his computer

Los niños se pusieron enfermos despues de caminar en frío – The kids got ill after walking at cold

El cliente se puso contento de trabajar con nosotros – The client was happy to work with us

- **HACERSE** – to make oneself/to become. Literally this verb means "to make onseself something" and is used for voluntary changes, for example: in profession, occupation, identity.

Ismael se hizo maestro – Ismael became a teacher

Lucila no quiere hacerse comunista – Lucila doesn't want to become a communist

El vendedor esta haciendose muy rico – The vendor is getting very rich

- **LLEGAR A SER** – This construction also means "to become" and it highlights a result of a preceding action.

Ismael llegó a ser maestro despues de cuatro años de estudiar – Ismael became a teacher after four years of studying

Ojalá Carlos llegaré a ser periodista pronto – Hopefully Carlos will soon become a journalist

Carolina llegó a ser madre – Carolina became a mother

- **QUEDARSE** – to become in meaning of "to leave oneself to be", i.e. with permanent change

Pablo se quedó viejo – Pablo became old

Este cantante se ha quedado una leyenda para siempre – This singer has become a legend forever

Los teléfonos con los pulsadores van a quedarse olvidado pronto – Phones with buttons are going to be forgotten soon

The verb VOLVER

Initially the verb VOLVER means "to return". However this verb has other ways of use, and is used in some verbal constructions:

- **As it was said above, VOLVER means "to become", "to come back", "to get back"**

¿Cuándo volverás? – When you come back?

Tenemos que volver a casa – We have to get back home

No necesito que ella me vuelva nada – I don't need her to return me anything

- **VOLVER A + INFINITIVE means "again", i.e. "to do something again".**

If VOLVER means "to return", so the translation "again" in this construction should have the logical sense as "return to do something again".

Mi abuela volvió a preguntarme – My grandma asked me again

¡Yo no volverá a contestar su cuestiónes! – I won't answer your questions again!

Ellos volverán a competir pronto – They will compete again soon

- **VOLVER + DIRECT OBJECT – to turn something (over)**

Antonio volvió el auto al lado y aparcó en el borde de la carretera – Antonio turned the car aside and parked in the roadside

¿Si tú vuelves las paginas tan rápido, cuántos palabras puedes leer por un minuto? – If you turn pages so fast, how any words can you read for one minute?

Despues de ese evento, él volvió su vida a otra dirección – After that event he turned his life to another direction

- **VOLVERSE**

This way of saying "to become" was already considered in the previous section.

The verb DEJAR

DEJAR is very commonly used verb, its basic translation is "to leave", however it has many variations of its basic translation. This verb is regular.

- **DEJAR – to leave (to place) something somewhere**

No dejes tu mochila aquí – Don't leave your backpack here

¿Quién dejo la leche en la mesa? – Who left the milk on the table?

Creo que dejé mi pasaporte en mi auto – I think that I left my passport in my car

- **DJAR – to delay, to postpone, to leave for later**

¡No deje la cura para luego! – Don't leave the cure for later! (formal)

¿Por qué tu tía dejaba su visita hasta tan muchos veces hasta hoy? – Why your aunt delayed her visit so many times until today?

Chicos, dejenlo para mañana – Guys, leave it for tomorrow

- **DEJAR – to allow/to let**

¡Dejame it! – Let me go!

¡Dejale decir que ella quiere decir! – Let her say what she wants to say!

El controlador de cara nos dejó entrar – The face controller allowed us to come in

- **DEJAR – to leave alone**

¡Dejame por favor! Estoy muy ocupado! – Leave me alone, please! I am very busy!

Olvídalo y déjalo – Forget it and leave him alone

Vamos a dejarlo y volver a otro tema – Let's leave it alone and turn to another subject

- **DEJAR – to pass on, to give, to leave for somebody**

¿Me dejarás tu número de teléfono? – Will you give me your phone number?

Déjenos su contactos antes de Usted salga – Give us your contacts before you leave

A pesar de estando enojado, Felipe nos dejo un poco dinero – Despite of being angry, Philip gave us some money

- **DEJAR DE – to stop doing something, to quit, to give up to do something, to abandon**

¿Tú me quieres que deje de bailar con otras mujeres? – You want me to stop dancing with other women?

¿Cuándo Usted dejaré de llegar tarde? – When you stop coming late?

Su novio no quiere dejar de fumar – Her boyfriend doesn't want to give up smoking

- **DEJAR QUE – to wait until something**

Dejamos que obtengamos el dinero – We wait until we get money

¿Quién va a dejar que el Bitcoin se caiga? – Who is going to wait until Bitcoin falls down?

No deja que el momento perfecto venga – Don't wait until the perfect moment come

- **DEJAR + ADJECTIVE/PARTICIPLE – to leave something/somebody in certain state**

El entrenamiento les dejo contento a todos – The training left everyone happy

Un viaje a Georgia dejará indiferente a nadie – A trip to Georgia will not leave anybody indifferent

El curso de Inglés le dejó satisfecho a Valentina – The course of English left Valentina satisfied

LOGRAR, CONSEGUIR, ALCANZAR – to achieve/reach/get

These verbs have the same translations to English, however in Spanish they mean different kinds of those translations

- **LOGRAR – to achieve (verb), LOGRO – achievement (noun). This verb and noun describe an achievement that required an effort:**

¡Felicidades por este logro! (Por ejemplo terminar la Universidad) – Congratulations for this achievement! (for example, finishing University, because it requires an effort)

¿Qué haces para lograr tu objetivo? – What do you do to achieve your goal?

El científico he logrado mucho durante su carrera – The scientist achieved a lot during his career

- **ALCANZAR – to achieve/reach out. This verb has a physical meaning. I.e. – reach something physically, For example "Can you reach that branch of the tree by hand?":**

Alcanza esa manzana que está en la rama del árbol porque yo no la alcanzo – Reach out this apple that is in that branch of the tree because I don't reach it out

Alcánzame la botella que está en la estantería superior – Reach out the bottle that is on the top shelf

¿Usted puede ayudarme a alcanzar la maleta del ático? – Can you help me to reach out the suitcase from the attic?

- **CONSEGUIR – to achieve/reach/manage/to get something either with or without effort:**

Consiguió llegar temprano al trabajo a pesar de que salió tarde de su casa – He managed to get to work early despite he left home late

Ellos conseguirán un aumento de sueldo pronto – They will reach an increase de salary soon

Consiguió una casa en buena zona – He got a house in a good zone

REVISAR, COMPROBAR, VERIFICAR – to check

- **REVISAR – to check/to revise. This verb means "to check" in meaning of "to see again":**

Revisa el ejercicio de español que hiciste – Check the exercise of Spanish that you made

Revisalo otra vez por favor – Check it again please

No se puede revisarlo porque el acceso está bloqueado – One can't check it because the access is blocked

- **COMPROBAR – to check, literally "to do probes with". This verb means "to check" in meaning of "to do a small test between one thing and another". This verb has to be accompanied by what one must check.**

Comprueba como este anuncio se utiliza – Check how this ad works

¿Puede Usted comprobar su trabajo? – Can you check his work?

Vamos a comprobar como este producto se vende en la tienda online – Let's check how this product is sold in the online store

- **VERIFICAR – to check/verify. This verb is used to prove that something is right.**

Verifica que trago está llena en tu copa – Check which drink is in your cup

Se podría verificar si él les dijese eso – One could check if he said that to them

La tarea terminada requiere la verificación – The finished task requires verification

TRAER and LLEVAR – to bring

The illustration shows the difference between these verbs.

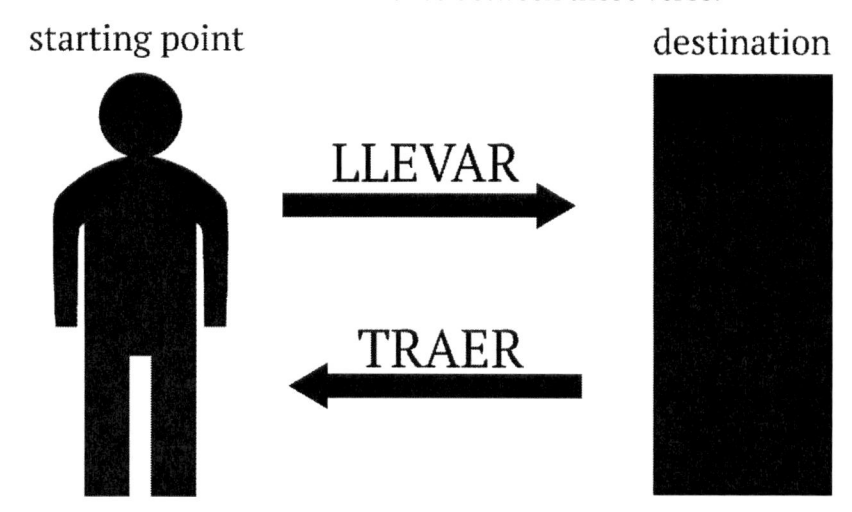

starting point　　　　　　　　　destination

LLEVAR →

← TRAER

- **LLEVAR - to bring to, to carry**

El cartero llevará la carta a la dirección – The postman will bring the letter to the address

Llevale mi regalo a tu padre por favor – Bring my gift for your father to him please

¡No lleves tus zapatos sucios a la habitación! – Don't bring your dirty shoes to the room!

- **TRAER – to bring from**

Trae agua de la cocina – Bring water from the kitchen

Tráeme un poco de té por favor – Bring me some tea please

Las turistas traían hongos del bosque muchos veces – Tourists brought mushrooms from the forest many times

SABER and CONOCER

There is only one verb "to know" in English, but in Spanish there are two – SABER and CONOCER. Despite they both can mean "to know", they are different.

- **Saber - to know something as a fact or information, to know something about the subject (i.e. to know a language)**

¿Que sabes sobre el horario nuevo – What do you know about the new schedule?

¿Dónde está la estación de metro? Yo no sé – Where is the metro station? I don't know

No supimos nada acerca de eso – We didn't know anything about that

- **Saber – to know how to do something (and be able to do that),**

Es buenísimo que Usted sabe bailar tango – It is great that you know how to dance tango

¿Quién de vosotros sabe reparar las bicicletas? – Who of you knows how to repair bicycles?

El diseñador sabe dibujar la infografía – The designer knows how to draw infographics

- **Conocer – to know someone or something or a place that one is familiar with**

Conozco tu país muy bien – I know your country very good

Laura aún no conoce a nadie en la escuela nueva – Laura doesn't know anyone in the new school yet

Yo conocía a un buen fotógrafo pero perdió su contactos – I knew a good photographer but I lost his contacts

- **Conocer(se) – to meet (for the first time)**

Nos conocimos en la expoición – We met in the exhibition

En la Universidad yo conocí a algunos amigos – I met some friends in the university

El viajero conoció a mucha gente durante sus viajes – The traveler met a lot of people during his trips

TOMAR and SACAR

Both of these verbs are translated to English as "to take". However they are different. Here is an illustration:

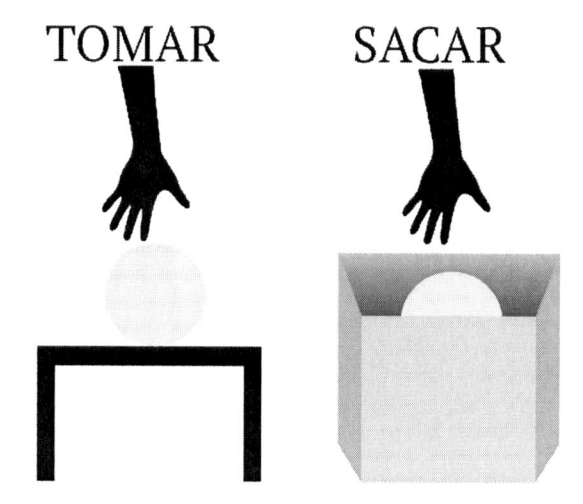

- **TOMAR – to take**

Tomalo al avión – Take it to the airplane

Toma la cerveza – Take the beer

Quiero tomar algo para comer – I want to take something to eat

- **SACAR – to take out**

Saca las cosas del paquete – Take the things out of pack

Saca el dinero de la billetera – Take money out of the wallet

Mi hijo sacó la ropa para el invierno de la despensa – My son took winter clothes from the storeroom

Build sentences with these words:

el parque – park	la clave – key
el gimnasio – gym	el teclado – keyboard
la frontera – border	la basura – rubbish
alto – high/tall	necesario – necessary
el ingreso – income	la mente – mind
el gasto – spending	el red social – social network
la capacidad – capacity	último – last
la falta - lack	cantidad – quantity/amount

Lesson 21: Greetings and goodbyes

How to say "Hello", "Good morning/afternoon/evening/night":

Hola! – Hello, hi

Buenos días – Good morning

Buenas tardes – Good afternoon

Buenas noches – Good night, good evening

How to say "How are you?":

¿Cómo estás? – How are you? (informal, singular)

¿Cómo está? – How are you? (Formal, singular)

¿Cómo están? – How are you? (Formal, plural)

¿Cómo estáis? – How are you? (Informal, plural; used only in Spain)

¿Qué tal? – How it is going?

¿Cómo te va? – How is it going?

¿Qué pasa? – What's up?/What's happening?

¿Qué estás haciendo? – What are you doing?

How to say "Well, thanks":

Bien, gracias – Well, thanks

Muy bien – Very well

Mal – bad

Así-así – so-so

Más o menos – so-so

De nada – You're welcome

How to say "Goodbye":

Adiós – Goodbye

Nos vemos – See you

Nos vemos la próxima vez – See you next time

Chao – bye

Que tengas un buen día – Have a good day

Another way to say "Goodbye" is to say it with HASTA which means "until", but in goodbyes it means "see you ... (until when?)":

Hasta luego – See you later

Hasta pronto – See you soon

Hasta mañana – See you tomorrow

Hasta la vista – Until next meeting

Example of a short dialogue:

- Hola, ¿Cómo estás? – Hello, how are you?

- Muy bien, gracias. ¿Y tú? – Very well, thanks, and you?

- Yo tambien. ¿Qué vas a hacer hoy? – Me too, what are you going to to today?

- Despues del trabajo voy a ir a la tienda a comprar algunas cosas y entonces iré a casa y descansaré – After work I am going to go to the store, buy some things and then go home and relax

- Creo que voy a hacer lo mismo. ¡Qué tengas un buen día! ¡Hasta el fin de semana! – I think I am going to do the same. Have a good day! See you in the weekend!

- Gracias amigo. ¡Hasta luego! – Thank you friend, see you soon!

Lesson 22: Thanks and apologizes

Gracias – thank you, thanks.

Muchas gracias – thank you a lot

Gracias por … - Thank you for …

De nada – You're welcome

- ¡Muchas gracias por tu ayuda, mi amiga! – Thank you a lot for your help, my friend!

- ¡De nada! -You're welcome!

Disculpar – to apologize, to excuse

Disculpe (command Usted), **Disculpa** (command tú) – Excuse me/I am sorry. This word is used in formal situations, when you want to ask something, or when you want to apologize in minor situations.

Disculpe, ¿Dónde está la plaza? - Excuse me, where is the square?

¡Disculpa! – I am sorry (for example, if you bumped somebody accidentally)

Also one can say:

Discúlpeme/Discúlpame – I am sorry/Exuse me

Disculparse – to apologize

Me disculpo por lo que occurrió ayer – I apologize for what happened yesterday

Javier se disculpó por su compartamiento – Javier apologized for his behavior

Estoy seguro que él no se disculpará – I am sure that he will not apologize

Perdonar – to forgive, to excuse. This verb can be use used in the same way as Disculpar, and also as "to forgive".

Perdóname por favor! – Forgive me please!

Después de muchos años él perdonó a su hijo – After many years he forgave his son

Perdón – I am sorry/ Excuse me/ Pardon. This word is used as apologize in minor situations, and also can be used the same way as Disculpe

¡Perdón! ¿Dónde está el hotel? – Excuse me, where is the hotel?

¡Perdón! – I am sorry (for example, if you bumped somebody accidentally, as well as Disculpa/Disculpe)

Also, one can say:

Perdóneme/Perdóname – I am sorry/Excuse me, and also it means "Forgive me".

¡Perdóname, mi querido! – Forgive me, my dear!

Lo siento – I am sorry. This phrase is used in more serious and emotional situations that disculpe and perdón. For example:

Lo siento por mi mal error – I am sorry for my bad mistake

Lo siento mucho, esto es mi culpa – I am very sorry, this is my fault

Ayer no tuve el tiempo de visitarte, lo siento – Yesterday I didn't have time to visit you, I am sorry

Lo lamento – I am sorry. This phrase is used to describe a deep regret. One can use it instead of *lo siento* in order

Lo lamento que lo olvidé – I am sorry that I forgot it/I regret that I forgot it

Lo lamento mucho que no te llame a la fiesta – I am very sorry that I didn't call you to the party

Lo lamento pero eso no depende de nosotros – I am sorry, but that does not depend on us

Lesson 23: How to tell about yourself

Mi nombre es ... – my name is ...;

Yo soy ... – I am ...

Soy de – I am from ...

Tengo ... años – I am ... years old (In Spanish it literally means "I have ... years")

Vivo en ... - I live in ...

Yo estudio en ... - I study in ...

Yo estudio ... (qué?) – I study ... (what?)

Yo trabajo como ... – I work as ...

Yo trabajo por ... – i work for ...

Me gusta ... (qué? Qué hacer?) – i like ... (what? To do what?)

Yo hago ... - I do ...

Mis pasatiempos son .... – My hobbies are ...

Me gusta ... – I like ...

Yo hablo Español, Inglés, Francés y otros idiomas extranjeros – I speak Spanish, English, French and other foreign languages

Yo aprendo ... – I learn ...

Yo quiero ... – I want ....

Yo estoy casado – I am married

Yo estoy soltero – I am single

Tengo una esposa/un marido – I have a wife/husbant

Tengo dos hijos/hijos/hijas – I have two children/sons/daughters

Tengo un hermano/una Hermana – I have a brother/a sister

Lesson 24: How to tell time and date?

The main thing to memorize here is that number of an hour will be with a <u>feminine</u> article (la, las), because it means "it is one hour", where "hour" is hidden, e.g. Es la una (hora). Hora – feminine noun.

Es la una – it is 1 o'clock

Es la una y cinco – it is 1:05

After 1, numbers become plural:

Son las dos – it is 2 o'clock

Son las tres – it is 3 o'clock

Also

…. y media …. – half past …

Son las dos y media – it is half past two (2:30)

… y cuarto – it is quarter past …

Son las diez y cuarto – It is quarter past ten (10:15)

Son las tres menos diez – it is 2:50/it is 3 without 10, that literally means "it is 3:00 minus 00:10".

Son las cuatro menos cuatro – it is 3:56 (it is 4 without 4)

Salimos a las ocho – we leave at 8

Vendremos a las cinco - we will come at 5

How to say "At … o'clock"

In order to say "at … o'clock ….", use the template:

$$A\ las\ ....\ DE\ ....$$

A las cinco **de** la mañana – At 5 o'clock in the morning

A las ocho **de** la tarde – At 8 p.m.

A las nueve – At 9 o'clock

A las dos y media **de** la noche – At half past four at night

A la una y veinte cinco – At 1:25

How to tell a date?

In order to tell a date in Spanish, all you need to know is numbers. Check the chapter "DICTIONARY: numerals". And here is how to connect the numbers to dates:

Day DE month DE year

And memorize Months:

Enero – January

Febrero – February

Marzo – March

Abril – April

Mayo – May

Junio – June

Julio – July

Agosto – August

Septiembre – September

Octubre – October

Noviembre – November

Let's say "May 5th of 2012" (**5.05.2012**): cinco de mayo de dos mil doce;

And more examples:

8.10.1921 – Ocho de octubre de mil novecientos veinte uno;

1.01.2014 – Uno de enero de dos mil catorce –

Today is **04.01.2017** - Hoy es el cuatro de enero de dos mil diecisiete

15.11.2016 – Quince de noviembre de dos mil dieciséis

Lesson 25: Summarizing, vocabulary learning tips and what to do further

The previous 24 lessons walked you through all subjects of essential grammar that you need to know to connect words into phrases and build any sentences that your vocabulary allows you to.

We learned all we need to know about verbs, about nouns and adjetives and about pronouns, considered some how to's and increased vocabulary. If you learned attentively and applied it in practice, all you need further is to gain vocabulary and improve perception of live speech.

Now I want to give my personal tips on how to learn vocabulary and understand what you listen as fast as possible. I don't insist that they are useful for anybody, but some of them should definitely be helpful to you.

5 tips on faster vocabulary memorization:

1. Learn new words in context. Write down new words on paper and write some sentences that contain all of them, and read them aloud until you memorize these new words.

2. Use the method of associations. Write a word, draw lines to word-associations to this word. Also you can draw tiny pictures in order to memorize it visually. In the illustration you can see association chains from the word *la ciudad – city*.

3. Most of adjetives have antonyms. Use them to learn adjectives in pairs with antonyms, and memorize two words at the same time.

4. You can form up to 1000 phrases out of 10 words. Write down 10 new words and form as many sentences out of them as you need to memorize these 10 words.

5. Sticky notes or small papers. Write new words on sticky notes and stick on your computer so that you will periodically move eyes to it. Or put small papers on the table next to your computer and periodically move your eyes to them. And change them as soon as you memorize them.

How to perceive live speech?

- Listen passively doing other tasks. The benefit of passive listening is a debatable thing, however personally for me it works. There are tons of videos with excellent pronunciation in Youtube. I recommend to listen something you are interested in, so you will perceive words and phrases faster.

- Pronounce words and phrases aloud, louder than you usually talk. It will improve your pronunciation skills and skills of voice perception.

- Listen non-passively, find podcasts or even better podcasts with transcripts. Listen a podcast, then read transcript, then listen again.

- Watch movies that you already watched in your native language. If you watch what you remember, you will comprehend the words and phrases that you already heard in your native language combined with visual moving image. And turn off subtitles. If you see subtitles – you don't pay attention to speech, subtitles are written not for language learners.

- Listen and translate songs. You probably listen favorite songs over and over more than one time, and more than one hundred times. This is a great opportunity for learning language. If you read the lyrics and translate them, you will hear them over and over again, and will perceive them in songs and in live speech.

What to do further?

Apply just learned things on practice. Find study buddies and native speakers to talk to. In the chapter *Additional content > Links* you will find links to online chats where you can find someone to talk to. Practice as much as possible, try to think in Spanish language instead of your native one, create artificial immersion into Spanish, and you will get fluent as soon and fast as possible.

Additional Content

PHRASEBOOK

Frases communes – *Common phrases*

¿Qué tal?/¿Cómo estás? – How are you? (informal)

¿Cómo está Usted? – How are You? (formal)

¿Bien, y tu? – I am fine, and you? (informal)

¿Bien, y Usted? – I am fine, and you? (formal)

¡Gracias! – Thank you!

¡De nada! – You're welcome!

Sí – Yes

No – No

¡Adios! – Good bye!/Bye!

¡Hasta luego! – See you soon

¡Hasta la vista! – Good bye!(Until the meeting!)

¡Disculpe! – Excuse me!

¡Lo siento! – I am sorry!

¡Salud! – Cheers!

¿Cómo te llamas? – What is your name? (informal)

¿Cómo se llama Usted? – What is your name? (formal)

Me llamo… – My name is…

¡Encantado(a) de conocerte! – Nice to meet you!

¿De dónde eres? – Where are you from? (informal)

¿De dónde es Usted? – Where are you from? (formal)

Soy de… – I am from…

¿Cuántos años tienes? – How old are you? (informal)

¿Cuántos años tiene Usted? – How old are you? (formal)

Tengo … años – I am… years old

¿Qué haces en la vida? – What do you do in life? (informal)

¿Qué hace Usted en la vida? – What do you do in life? (formal)

¿Dónde estudias? – Where do you study? (informal)

¿Dónde estudia Usted? – Where do you study? (formal)

¿Qué estudias? – What do you study? (informal)

¿Qué estudia Usted? – What do you study? (formal)

¿Tú hablas Español/Ingles? – Do you speak Spanish/English? (informal)

¿Habla Usted Español/Ingles? – Do you speak Español/English? (formal)

¿Qué significa …? – What means …?

¿Cómo decir …? – How to say …?

¿Qué hora es? – What time is it?

Son las cinco – (five) o'clock

Las compras y dinero – *Shopping and money*

¿Cuánto cuesta? – How much is?

Yo quisiera… – I would like

¿Acepta Usted las tarjetas? – Do you accept cards?

Por favor – Please

¿Puedo verlo? – Can I see it?

Es demasiado caro – It is too expensive

¿Dónde puedo intercambiar dinero? – Where can I exchange money?

El transporte – *Transport*

Boleto por un paseo – One ride ticket

Boleto por dos paseos – Two rides ticket

Buleto por noventa minutos – A ticket for 90 minutes

Boleto por un día – A ticket for one day (for 24 hours)

Boleto por dos días – A ticket for two days (for 48 hours)

¿Cuánto cuesta el boleto a …? – How much is a ticket to …?

Billete de ida por favor – One-way ticket please

Billete redondo por favor – Both ways ticket please

Autobús – Bus

Trolebús – Trolleybus

Tranvía – Tram

Metro – Metro/subway/tube

El tren de cercanías – Commuter train

Tren – Train

Avión – Airplane

Coche – Car

Taxi – Taxi

¿Cómo llegar a …? – How to get to …?

Quisiera rentar un coche/bicicleta – I would like to rent a car/bicycle

La comida – *Food*

¿Qué platos nacionales hay aquí? – What national dishes there are here?

Una cerveza/un café/un té por favor – Beer/coffee/tea please

¿Puedo tener la cuenta? – May I have a bill?

¡Muy delicioso! – Very tasty!

¡Soy alérgico a … ! – I am allergic to…

Direcciones – *Directions*

Es a la izquerda/a la derecha/adelante/en la esquina – It is left/right/straight ahead/at the corner

¿Qué tan lejos está ...? – How far is ...?

¿Dónde está el banco/cajero automatico/oficina postal/oficina de cambio – Where is a bank/cash machine/post office/exchange office?

¿Dónde está la información turística? – Where is tourist information?

¿Puede Usted mostrarlo en el mapa? – Can you show in on the map?

Dondé está el consulado/la embajada? – Where is the embassy/consulate?

Alojamiento – *Accomodation*

Tengo la reservación – I have a reservation

¿Tiene Usted la habitación individual/doble? – Do you have a single/double room available?

Quiería quedarme aquí por ... noches – I would like to stay for... nights

Salud y emergencias – *Health and emergencies*

¡Ayuda! – Help!

Necesito un doctor / dentist / policía – I need a doctor/dentist/policeman

¿Hay una farmacia cerca de aquí? – Is there a pharmacy nearby?

!Llame a la ambulancia / policia! – Call the ambulance/police!

Verbs that require prepositions

A + infinitive:	A + object
Aprender a – to learn to	Acercarse a – to approach
Aydar a – to help to	Asistir a – to attend
Alcanzar a – to manage to	Aspirar a – to aspire
Animar a – to encourage to	Contribuir a – to contribute to
Empezar a – to begin/to start to	Entrar a – to enter
Comenzar a – to begin/to start to	Jugar a – to play
Enseñar a – to teach to	Querer a – to love to
Echar a – to start/begin to	Responder a – to respond to
Echarse a – to start/begin to	Sonar a – to sound like
Ponerse a – to begin to	Subir a – to get on
Invitar a – to invite to	Oler a – to smell like
Atreverse a – to dare	Dirigirse a – to address
Saber a – to taste like to	Venir a – to come to
Acostumbrarse a – to get used to	Salir a – to leave to
Decidirse a – to decide to	
Dedicarse a – to devote oneself to	
Llegar a – to succeed in	
Negarse a – to refuse to	
Obligar a – to force to, to obligate to	
Ir a – to go to/to be going to	
Apresurarse a – to hurry to	
Forzar a – to force to	
Bajar a – to go down to	
Conducir a – to lead to	
Impular a – to urge to	
Llegar a ser – to become	
Resistirse a – to resist to	

| Volver a – to ___ again | |

En + infinitive:	En + object
Consentir en – to consent to	Consistir en – to consist of
Convenir en – to agree to	Confiar en – to trust
Convenir en – to agree to	Insistir en – to insist on
Quedar en – to agree to	

Con + infinitive	Con + object
Divertirse con – to enjoy	Casarse con – to marry
Contar con – to count/rely on	Encontrarse con – to meet
Amenazar con – to threaten to	Enfrentarse con – to face
Contentarse con – to be satisfied with	Pagar con – to pay by
	Quedarse con – to keep
	Soñar con – to dream about

De + infinitive	De + object
Acabar de – to have just ___ (done sth.)	Acusar de – to accuse of
	Abusar de – to abuse
Acordarse de – to remember to	Alejarse de – to go away from
Cansarse de – to get tired of	Depender de – to depend on
Terminar de – to stop/finish	Servir de – to serve as
Tartar de – to try to	Reírse de – to laugh at
Dejar de – to stop/give up	Vestir de – to dress in
Olvidarse de – to forget to	Disfrutar de – to enjoy
Parar de – to stop	Cubrir de – to cover with
	Pensar de – to think about
	Quejarse de – to complain about

Por + infinitive	Por + object
Acabar por – to end up (doing something)	Cambiar por – to change for
Terminar por – to end up (doing something)	Estar por – to be in favor of
	Jurar por – to swear on
Disculparse por – to apologize for	Preocuparse por – to worry about
Luchar por – to struggle for	Rezar por – to pray for
Estar por – to be in favor of	Salir por – to leave by
	Votar por – to vote for
	Tomar por – to take for
	Interesarse por – to be interested in

Vocabulary: NUMERALS

0	cero	1st	primero
1	uno	2nd	segundo
2	dos	3rd	tercero
3	tres	4th	cuarto
4	cuatro	5th	quinto
5	cinco	6th	sexto
6	seis	7th	séptimo
7	siete	8th	octavo
8	ocho	9th	noveno
9	nueve	10th	décimo
10	diez	11th	undécimo
11	once	12th	duodécimo
12	doce	13th	decimotercero
13	trece	14th	decimocuarto
14	catorce	15th	decimoquinto
15	quince	16th	decimosexto
16	dieciséis	17th	decimoséptimo
17	diecisiete	18th	decimoctavo
18	dieciocho	19th	decimonoveno
19	diecinueve	20th	vigésimo
20	veinte	21st	vigésimo primero
21	veinte uno	22nd	vigésimo segundo
22	veinte dos	23rd	vigésimo tercero
23	veinte tres	24th	vigésimo cuarto
24	veinte cuatro	25th	vigésimo quinto
25	veinte cinco	30th	trigésimo
26	vente seis	40th	cuadragésimo
27	veinte siete	50th	quincuagésimo
28	veinte ocho	60th	sexagésimo
29	veinte nueve	70th	septuagésimo
30	treinta	80th	octogésimo
40	cuarenta	90th	nonagésimo
50	cincuenta	100th	centésimo
60	sesenta	1000th	milésimo
70	setenta	10.000th	diez milésimo
80	ochenta	1.000.000th	millonésimo
90	noventa	1.000.000.000th	billonésimo

100	ciento	1.000.000.000.000th	trillonésimo
110	ciento diez		
120	ciento veinte		
200	doscientos		
300	trescientos		
400	cuatrocientos		
500	quinientos		
600	seiscientos		
700	setecientos		
800	ochocientos		
900	novecientos		
1000	mil		
1100	mil cien		
10.000	diez mil		
1.000.000	millón		
2.000.000	dos millones		
1.000.000.000	billón		
1.000.000.000.000	trillón		

Vocabulary: VERBS

to achieve	lograr, alcanzar	to look	mirarse
to act	actuar	to look at	mirar
to adore	adorar	to love	amar
to answer	contestar	to mean	significar
to appear	aparecer	to meet	reunirse, conocer
to arrive	llegar	to memorize	memorizar
to ask	preguntar	to mention	mencionar
to asume	asumir	to move	mover, moverse
to attempt	intentar	to offend	ofender
to avoid	evitar	to offer	ofrecer
to awake	despertarse	to open	abrir
to be	ser, estar	to pass	pasar
to become	volverse	to pay	pagar
to believe	creer	to ask for	pedir
to belong	pertenecer a	to play	jugar
to blame	culpar	to pray	orar, rezar
to boil	hervir	to prepare	preparar
to breathe	respirar	to print	imprimir
to buy	comprar	to promise	prometer
to call	llamar	to punish	castigar
to carry, bring	llevar	to put	poner
to celebrate	celebrar	to quit	dejar
to check	comprobar, revisar, verificar	to receive	recibir
to close	cerrar	to rejoice	alegrarse
to come	llegar, venir	to relax	relajarse
to compare	comparar	to remember	recordar
to complete	cumplir	to repair	reparar
to consider	considerar	to resistir	resist
to continue	continuar	to return	volver
to cost	costar	to ride	montar
to count	contar	to rise	subir
to create	crear	to run	correr

to cry	llorar	to satisfy	satisfacer
to cut, crop	cortar	to save	guardar
to dance	bailar	to save (money)	ahorrar
to decrease	disminuir	to say	decir
to define	definir	to search	buscar
to depart	salir	to see	ver
to describe	describir	to sell	vender
to determine	determinar	to send	enviar, mandar
to die	morir	to share	compartir
to disappear	desaparecer	to silence	silenciar
to disappoint	decepcionar	to sing	cantar
to discuss	discutir	to sit	sentar
to do	hacer	to sleep	dormir
to draw	dibujar	to smell	oler
to dream	soñar	to smile	sonreír
to drink	beber	to solve	resolver
to drive	conducir, manejar	to sound	sonar
to eat	comer	to speak	hablar
to enjoy	disfrutar	to spend (money)	gaster (el dinero)
to envy	envidiar	to spend (time)	pasar (el tiempo)
to exist	existir	to stand	estar de pie
fto all	caer	to start, begin	comenzar, empezar
fto all asleep	dormirse	to stop, finish	terminar, acabar
to fall in love	enamorarse de	to study	estudiar
to feel	sentirse	to suffer	sufrir
to find	encontrar	to swim	nadar
to fix	fijar	to take	tomar
to fly	volar	to talk	conversar
to focus	enfocar	to teach	enseñar
to follow	seguir	to tell	contar
to forget	olvidar	to think	pensar
to forgive	perdonar	to translate	traducir

to get	obtener, conseguir	to travel	viajar
to get tired	cansarse	to try	tratar
to get used	acostumbrarse a	to use	usar, utilizar
to give	dar	to visit	visitar
to give up	dejar de	to wait	esperar
to go	ir	to wake up	despertarse
to go out	salir	to want	querer
to guess	adivinar	to warm, heat	calentar
to hate	odiar	to wash	lavar
to have	tener	to wear	vestir
to hear	oír	to wish	desear
to help	ayudar	to work	trabajar
to hit	golpear	to write	escribir
to hold	sostener	to launch	lanzar
to hope	esperar	to fail	fracasar
to hug	abrazar	to perceive	percibir
to hurry	apresurarse	to smell	oler
to increase	aumentar, incrementar	to advice	aconsejar
to invite	invitar	to bring	traer
to involve	involucrar	to throw	tirar
to jump	saltar	to research	investigar
to keep	mantener	to lend	prestar
to kill	matar	to borrow	pedir prestado
to kiss	besar	to marry	casarse
to know	saber, conocer	to worry	preocuparse
to learn	aprender	to trust	confiar
to lie	mentir	to hesitate	vacilar
to lie down	acostarse	to thank	agradecer
to like	gustar	can	poder
to listen	escuchar	must	deber
to live	vivir	to owe	deber

Vocabulary: NOUNS

El humano	**Human**	**El país**	**Country**
el hombre	man	Rusia	Russia
la mujer	woman	Estados Unidos de America	United States of America
el niño	(little) boy	Brasil	Brasil
la niña	(little) girl	Alemania	Germany
el chico	Boy, guy	Francia	France
la chica	girl	Inglaterra	England
		Gran Bretaña	Great Britain
La familia	**Family**	Canadá	Canada
los padres	parents	Polonia	Poland
el padre, papá	father, dad	República Checa	Czech Republic
la madre, mamá	mother, mom	Eslovaquia	Slovakia
la abuela	grandma	Serbia	Serbia
el abuelo	grandad	Hungría	Hungary
los niños	children	Croacia	Croatia
el hijo	son	Turquía	Turkey
la hija	daughter	España	Spain
el hermano	brother	China	China
la hermana	sister	Australia	Australia
la tía	aunt	Nueva Zelanda	New Zealand
el tío	uncle	Méjico	Mexico
el sobrino	nephew	Eurasia	Eurasia
el cuñada	brother in law	Europa	Europe
la cuñada	sister in law	Asia	Asia
el relativo	relative	América	America
el marido	husband	África	Africa
la mujer	wife	Sudamérica/ América del Sur	South America
		Norteamérica/ América del Norte	North America
Casa	**Home, house**	Belarús	Belarus
el apartamento	flat, apartment	Suecia	Sweden
la habitación	room	Suiza	Switzerland
la cocina	kitchen	Austria	Austria
la bañera	bath	Finlandia	Finland

el baño	WC
la sala	living room
el balcón	balcony
el techo	ceiling
el tejado	roof
la puerta	door
el teléfono	phone
el sofá	sofa
la mesa	table
la silla	chair

Trabajo — **Work, job**

el negocio	business
la profeción	profession
la posición	position
el lucro	profit
el salario	salary, wage
los ingresos	revenue
el impuesto	tax
la oficina	office
la fábrica	factory
la empresa	enterprise
el jefe	boss
el trabajador	worker
el contador	accountant
el manager	manager
el director	director
el emprendedor	entrepreneur

Los estudios — **Studies**

la universidad	university
el instituto	institute
la academia	Academy
el colegio	college
la escuela	school
los cursos	courses
el estudiante	student

Noruega	Norway
Lituania	Lithuania
Letonia	Latvia
Rumania	Romania
Israel	Israel
Italia	Italy
Grecia	Greece
India	India
Montenegro	Montenegro
Egipto	Egypt
Ucrania	Ukraine
Camboya	Cambodia
Tailandia	Thailand
Filipinas	Phillipines
Corea	Corea
Arabia Saudita	Saudi Arabia
Chile	Chile
Tierra Verde	Greenland
Suecia	Sweden

La nacionalidad — **Nationality**

Ruso	Russian
Ukranio	Ukrainian
Belaruso	Belorussian
Brasileño	Brasilian
Americano	American
Inglés	Englishman
Francés	French
Alemano	German
Judio	Jew
Australiano	Australian
Chino	Chinese
Italiano	Italian
Checo	Czech
Húngaro	Hungarian
Finlandés	Finn
Sueco	Swede

el profesor	professor	Noruego	Norwegian
el maestro	teacher	Lituano	Lithuanian
el grado	grade	Letón	Latvian
el departamento	department	Griego	Greek
la aula	classroom	Turco	Turk
los deberes	homework	Español	Spaniard
la práctica	practice	Canadiense	Canadian
libro de texto	textbook	Mexicano	Mexican
libro de ejercicios	exercise book	Mongol	Mongol
el bolígrafo	pen	Eslavo	Slav
el lápiz	pencil	Asiático	Asian
la calculadora	calculator	Africano	African
las matemáticas	maths	Europeo	European
la física	physics	Británico	British
el idioma	language	Indio	Indian
la ingeniería	engineering	Suizo	Swiss
la technología	technology	Austriatico	Australian
la economía	economy		
la programación	programming	**El viaje**	**Travel**
la medicina	medicine	la ruta	route
la logística	logistics	la carretera	road
las humanidades	humanities	el boleto	ticket
el arte	art	el hotel	hotel
la sociología	sociology	el hostal	hostel
la ciencia política	political science	la excursión	excursion
la ciencia	science	el paseo	walk
La investigación	research	la cámara fotográfica	photo camera
La biología	biology	la cámara de video	video camera
		la gira	tour
La política	**Politics**	la guía de turismo	tour-guide book
el presidente	president	la guía	guide
el zar	tzar		
el rey	king	**El clima**	**Weather**
la reina	queen	el sol	sun
al alcalde	mayor	el cielo	sky

141

el diputado	deputy	la lluvia	rain
el líder	leader	la tormenta	thunderstorm
el partido político	political party	la nieve	snow
el parlamento	parliament	la nube	cloud
el gobierno	government	la nevada	snowstorm
el congreso	congress	el viento	wind
la autoridad	authority		
la monarquía	monarchy	**El animal**	**Animal**
la república	republic	el gato	cat(male)
la democracia	democracy	la gata	cat(female)
la dictadura	dictatorship	el perro	dog(male)
los elecciones	elections	la perra	dog(female)
la unión	union	el caballo	horse
el acuerdo	agreement	el cerdo	pig
constitución	constitution	la vaca	cow
la soberanía	sovereignty	el toro	bull
el estado	state	el oso	bear
el país	country	el reno	reindeer
la nación	nation	el hámster	hamster
		el ratón	mouse
El dinero	**Money**	la rata	rat
la moneda	currency	el papagayo	parrot
el billete de banco	banknote	la oveja	sheep
la moneda	coin	el carnero	ram
la tarjeta de crédito	credit card	la cabra	goat
el banco	bank	la gallina	hen
el crédito	credit		
el cambio de moneda	currency exchange	**La religión**	**Religion**
el recibo	receipt	el Dios	God
el dólar	dollar	la fe	faith
el euro	euro	la iglesia	church
el oro	gold	el templo	temple
la plata	silver	la catedral	cathedral
la billetera	wallet	el Cristianismo	Christianity

la cuenta	bill	el Islam	Islam
la ruqieza	wealth	el Budismo	Buddhism
la fortuna	fortune	el Judaismo	Judaizm
		la oración	prayer
La ciudad	**City, town**	el sacerdote	priest
el centro	center	el mulá	mullah
la calle	street	el monje	monk
la avenida	avenue	el profeta	prophet
el bulevar	boulevard	la profecía	prophesy
el distrito	district	la Biblia	Bible
el barrio	neighbourhood	el Corán	Quaran
el parque	park	el icono	icon
la marca	landmark	la cruz	cross
el edificio	building	el milagro	miracle
la casa	house	el patriarca	patriarch
		la Ortodoxia	Orthodoxy
La comida	**Food**	el Catolicismo	Catholicism
el trago	drink	el Protestantismo	Protestantism
la cocina	kitchen	el Luteranismo	Lutheranism
el cafetería	cafe	el Chiíta	Shiite
el restaurante	restaurant	el Sunni	Sunni
el agua	water	el bautismo	baptizing
el té	tea	el servicio divino	divine service
el café	coffee	la candela	candle
el pan	bread		
la leche	milk	**El deporte**	**Sport**
la carne	meat	el fútbol	football
el pescado	fish	el baloncesto	basketball
el cerdo	pork	el voleibol	volleyball
la carne de vaca	beef	el juego	game
la brocheta	kebab	la pelota	ball
la comida rápida	fast food	los músculos	muscles
la patata	potato	el gimnasio	gym
el tomate	tomato	el jogging	jogging
el pepino	cucumber	el entrenamiento	training
la ensalada	salad	el boxeo	boxing
el plato	dish	la natación	swimming

la cerveza	beer		
el vino	wine	**El transporte**	**Transport**
el vodka	vodka	el auto	car
el conñac	cognac	el autobús	bus
el plato	plate	el tranvía	tram
la copa	cup	el metro	metro
el tenedor	fork	el tren	train
la cuchara	spoon	el tren de cercanías	commuter train
		el microbús	minibus
El tiempo	**Time**	el avión	airplane
el milenio	millenium	el helicóptero	helicopter
el siglo	century	el barco	ship
el año	year	el taxi	taxi
el mes	month	el camión	truck
la semana	week	la motocicleta	motorbike
el día	day	la bicicleta	bicycle
la hora	hour	el boleto	ticket
el minuto	minute	el pase	pass
la segunda	second	el conductor	driver
la historia	history	la parade de autobús	bus stop
el pasado	past	la estación	station
el presente	present	el aeropuerto	airport
el futuro	future	la estación de tren	train station
		el ferrocarril	railway
La música	**Music**	la carretera	road
la canción	song	la autopista	highway
la voz	voice	las carriles	rails
el cantante	singer	el horario	schedule
el instrumente musical	musical instrument		
la guitarra	guitar	**El ejército**	**Army**
el piano	piano	la guerra	war
el piano grande	grand piano	el soldado	soldier
el saxofón	saxophone	el general	general
el violín	violin	el tanque	tank
la trompeta	trumpet	la arma	weapon

el tambor	drum	la ametralladora	machine gun
el concierto	concert	el rifle	rifle
el artista	artist	la pistola	gun
el amor	love	el cochete	rocket
el alma	soul	La granada	grenade
el corazón	heart	la escuadra	squad
		las tropas	troops
		la bomba	bomb
		el bombardeo	bombing
		el ataque	attack
		la victoria	victory

Vocabulary: ADJECTIVES

another/other	otro	portuguese	portugués
abusive	abusivo	hot	caliente
active	activo	ignorant	ignorante
african	africano	impossible	imposible
alcohol	alcohólico	incredible	increíble
american	americano	independent	independiente
angry	enojado	japanese	japonés
annoying	molesto	jewish	judío
arabic	árabe	kind	amable, bueno
arrogant	arrogante	large, huge	grande, enorme
australian	australiano	late	tarde
bad	malo	latin	latín
beautiful	hermoso	left	izquierdo
big	grande, gran	light	claro
black	negro	light(weight)	ligero
blue	azul	long	largo
brasilian	brasileño	loud	ruidoso
brave	valiente	low	bajo
brown	marrón	medieval	medieval
canadian	canadiense	mexican	mexicano
cheap	barato	middle	medio
chinese	chino	narrow	estrecho, angosto
clean	limpio	northern	norteño
close	cercano	offensive	ofensivo
closed	cerrado	old	viejo, antiguo
cold	frío	open	abierto
colorful	vistoso	oppressive	opresivo
common	común	passive	pasivo
complete	completo	personal	personal
creative	creativo	pleasant	agradable
cute	lindo	polish	polaco
dangerous	peligroso	possible	posible

dark	oscuro	probable	probable
dear	querido	quiet	callado
dependent	dependiente	rainy	lluvioso
difficult	difícil	rare	raro
direct	directo	rich	rico
dirty	sucio	right	derecho
early	temprano	roman	romano
eastern	oriental	round	redondo
easy	fácil	russian	ruso
edible	comestible	safe	seguro
empty	vacío	saint	santo
English	Inglés	scandinavian	escandinavo
European	Europeo	shiny	brillante
evil	malvado	short	corto
expensive	costoso, caro	sick	enfermo
famous	famoso	silver	plateado
far	lejos	single	soltero
fast, quick	rápido	slim	delgado
fragile	frágil	slow	lento
french	francés	soft	suave
frequent	frecuente	southern	sureño
friendly	amistoso	spanish	español
frosty	escarchado	sporty	deportivo
full	completo	steel	acero
german	alemán	sunny	soleado
giant	gigante, gigantesco	sweet	dulce
golden	dorado	thick	grueso
good	bueno, buen	thin	delgado
greek	griego	unusual	raro
healthy	saludable	usual	usual
heavy	pesado	western	occidental
high, tall	alto	wide	amplio, ancho
poor	pobre	young	joven

147

Links

tools.verbix.com/webverbix/Spanish.html - the best Spanish verb conjugator. It has a lot of other languages apart from Spanish too.

hellolingo.com - language exchange chats.

interpals.net - international social network for language exchange and communication.

PlusSpeak.com – Author's website and blog.

• FREE BONUS •

Download your free copy of the book "How To Learn Any Language As Fast As Possible"

Download link: http://bit.ly/howtolearnlanguagesbook

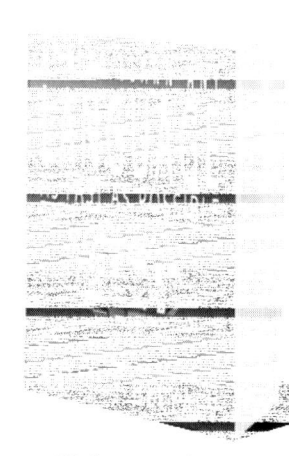

Do you want to get fluent fast, spend less time on learning and memorize more words?

This is a 42-page guide to efficient language learning with a lot of tips, tricks and techniques actively used by the author.

You will learn what a language consists of, how to build an effective learning algorithm of any language, the fastest ways to improve perceiving of speech, memorize more words and think in the target language.

Download your copy right now and never spend years for learning one language anymore!

You will be subscribed to a mailing list, if you don't want to receive further emails, you can unsubscribe any moment.

Manufactured by Amazon.ca
Acheson, AB